1 AND 2 THESSALONIANS

EPWORTH PREACHER'S COMMENTARIES

*

1 AND 2 THESSALONIANS

*

WILLIAM B. HARRIS
M.A., L.T.

LONDON : EPWORTH PRESS

SET IN MONOTYPE TIMES ROMAN AND PRINTED IN
GREAT BRITAIN BY THE CAMELOT PRESS LTD
LONDON AND SOUTHAMPTON

TO
My Wife

General Introduction

We are living in a day in which the authority and message of the Bible is being rediscovered and declared. Preachers are realizing afresh that their message must be based on the Word of God in Scripture. Many commentaries on the books of the Bible are already available, and give much space to the consideration of critical questions and historical and literary problems.

This new series of commentaries, as its name suggests, is written specifically for preachers, and particularly for those who feel themselves ill-equipped to study the more advanced works of scholarship. Its aim is to set forth the essential message of the Bible. Questions of authorship, date, background, will be dealt with briefly, and only in so far as they are necessary for informed preaching. The main purpose of each commentary will be (*a*) to explain the original meaning of each biblical passage, and (*b*) to indicate its relevance to human need in the present situation. Bearing in mind this dual purpose, each author will have freedom to use what method of treatment he thinks most suitable to the book of the Bible on which he is commenting.

To save space, the biblical text is not printed, but the commentary is based on that of the *Revised Version*.

The commentary on *1 and 2 Thessalonians* is by the Rev. William B. Harris who, since 1951, has been on the staff of the Tamilnad Theological College, Tirumaraiyur, South India. He is the author of commentaries on *Romans* and *1 Corinthians* (Christian Students Library) and *Ephesians* (ISPCK), and articles in the Tamil Theological Word Book.

'At first sight', he writes, 'most of the mighty themes of the gospel appear to be lacking in these epistles, apart from the "Second Coming", so unpalatable to modern ears and apparently so irrelevant.' But he shows, especially in the nineteen special *Notes* for preachers, how drastically this first impression must be revised.

GREVILLE P. LEWIS

Preface

THERE are many to whom I must say 'Thank-you'. First, I gladly acknowledge my indebtedness to the writers of the commentaries I have used—especially Rigaux, Masson, Oepke, Schlatter, Neil, Frame, Denney, Morris. I have also received valuable help from articles in Kittel's *Theologisches Wörterbuch*, and from Althaus's great book on Eschatology, *Die Letzten Dinge*. I should like to express my thanks to the Editor of this Series, the Rev. Greville P. Lewis, for the unfailing kindness and courtesy with which he did the work of editing; to him again and to the members of his committee, the Rev. Dr C. L. Mitton and Professor Kenneth Grayston, all of whom made many very valuable suggestions; also to the Rev. A. Raymond George, with whom I usefully discussed some of the Notes. But final decisions have been mine; I have no intention of making any of those named responsible for the imperfections and errors that still remain! Last, but by no means least, I must say 'Thank-you' to my wife, not only for the laborious work of typing and then re-typing the MS., but for much other help.

WILLIAM B. HARRIS

ABBREVIATIONS

RSV	*Revised Standard Version* (1952)
NEB	*New English Bible; New Testament* (1961)
CLM	C. Leslie Mitton, *St Mark* (E.P.C.)
AMW	A. Marcus Ward, *St Matthew* (E.P.C.)
OEE	Owen E. Evans, *St John* (E.P.C.)
VT	Vincent Taylor, *Romans* (E.P.C.)
KG	Kenneth Grayston, *Galatians, Philippians* (E.P.C.)
HKM	Harold K. Moulton, *Colossians, Ephesians* (E.P.C.)
RW	Ronald Williamson, *Hebrews* (E.P.C.)
GPL	Greville P. Lewis, *Johannine Epistles* (E.P.C.)
MHB	*Methodist Hymn-book* (1933)

N.B. Text references printed in heavy type relate to the particular Epistle (1 *or* 2 Thess) which is being studied.

Analysis of the Epistles and Table of Contents

THE FIRST EPISTLE TO THE THESSALONIANS

Introduction

THE Paul of the Thessalonian letters stands at about the mid-point of his missionary career. More than fifteen years before, on the Damascus road, he had been 'apprehended by Christ Jesus'. Now, as apostle to the Gentiles, he is at the height of his missionary powers. These letters may be, probably are, the first of his letters we possess. But let us not despise them as the first tentative efforts of a young missionary!

To grasp the letters for our preaching we must get the context clear. First we must follow Paul and his colleagues, Silas and Timothy, through the adventure of the 'second missionary journey'. We start with the 'drama of divine guidance' in Acts 16^{6-11}. Forbidden by the Holy Spirit to preach in Asia, not allowed by the Spirit of Jesus to enter Bithynia, they were led to Troas. There their obedience was rewarded by the vision which brought the gospel from Asia to Europe. The mission in Philippi (Acts 16^{12-40}) was marked by triumph, suffering and humiliation. In Acts 17^1 the faithful three travel on, filled with the divine courage described so vividly in 2^{1-12}, to—

Thessalonica

This city, capital of the Roman province of Macedonia and seat of the proconsul, was the sort of political and commercial centre Paul loved to claim for Christ. Its geographical position gave it an importance which, as Saloniki, second port of Greece, it has retained to the present day. A good harbour and a position on one of the great roads (the Via Egnatia) which led to Rome, put it in the centre of the busy traffic between the capital of the Empire and its eastern provinces. The citizens of Thessalonica were proud of their status as a 'free city' (a reward for political services rendered). They were governed by magistrates whom Luke, in the Greek text of Acts 17^{6-8}, calls 'politarchs'. (There was no evidence that Luke was right about this until inscriptions were discovered which proved that Macedonian magistrates were indeed called politarchs. A big feather in Luke the historian's cap!) As in other similar cities of the Empire, there were elements both favourable and unfavourable to the Pauline mission. There were plenty of people to listen to a preacher, but among them were 'the rabble' (Acts 17⁵). The wandering preacher was nothing new; indeed he was too familiar (2¹⁻¹²). There was an eager interest in religion, but much that passed in Thessalonica for religion was degrading and debased. There was a synagogue in which Paul could begin his work among Jews and 'devout Greeks' (i.e. pagans attracted to Jewish monotheism, though unready to pay the price of circumcision for the full Jewish faith), but how long was Jewish pride likely to tolerate the successful preaching of the Messiah the Jews had crucified? But if Paul's bold attempt to capture Thessalonica should, by the grace of God, succeed, how useful the city's lines of communication would be for the further spread of the gospel!

The Thessalonian Mission

Luke's account, in Acts 17¹⁻¹⁰, is very brief. If we take the 'we' of 16¹⁰, ¹¹, ¹², etc. as a sign of Luke's own presence in Philippi, we shall take the 'they' of 17¹ to mean that he was not himself present at Thessalonica. He records the mission in three little scenes.

Scene 1 (Acts 17¹⁻⁴). The synagogue. For three Sabbath days Paul interspersed Bible study on 'a suffering Messiah' with direct proclamation—'this Jesus, of whom I speak, *is* that Messiah'. The mission bore fruit—a few Jews, many from the 'devout-Greek fringe', and (Luke is interested to note) a good many women—and influential ones at that!

Scene 2 (Acts 17⁵⁻⁸). The Jews became violently jealous of the success of what they considered, understandably enough, to be Paul's 'sheep-stealing'. Their violence took two familiar forms —the hiring of agitators from among the rabble, and the framing of a false charge before the city 'politarchs'. The charge was no less than high treason. 'These that have turned the world upside down' (these dangerous revolutionaries) have a new king-emperor. (This shameless perversion of religious teaching about the Messiah into political crime was what Jesus also had suffered—see Luke 23[2]). In the non-availability of Paul and the others, the brunt of the trouble was borne by a certain Jason who had 'harboured' (*NEB*) Paul and his friends.

Scene 3 (Acts 17[9, 10]). The politarchs heard the case, 'bound over Jason and the others, and let them go' (*NEB*). The exact terms of this 'binding over' are not stated, but the situation was serious enough to demand the immediate departure of Paul and Silas (and presumably also Timothy, not mentioned in the account at all).

This account reads, plausibly enough, like three or four weeks of successful mission followed by a short, sharp crisis of opposition, and then departure. But some passages in Paul's letters make it necessary to modify this picture a little. 1[9] makes it clear that the majority of the Thessalonian believers had 'turned unto God from *idols*'. This does not fit the converts of Acts 17[4]. In Phil 4[16] Paul says 'even in Thessalonica ye (i.e. the Philippian believers) sent once and again unto my need' ('not once but twice over', *NEB*). This surely demands a longer time in Thessalonica than Acts 17[1–10] allows. We must therefore insert, between Scene 1 and Scene 2 above, a further 'Scene 1a'—a successful mission to Gentiles, lasting perhaps several months. This is not a reflection on Luke's accuracy, but rather an illustration on his frequent tendency to concentrate on the beginnings and ends of Pauline missions.

From Thessalonica to 1 Thessalonians

We must follow Paul a little further, as briefly as we can. After Thessalonica, Beroea. But there eager Bible-study was interrupted by further trouble-making from the Thessalonian Jews. So Paul moved on to Athens, leaving Silas and Timothy at Beroea; then urgently requesting them to come on to Athens. At Athens he preached his famous 'sermon to philosophers', and left soon after for Corinth. We get a glimpse from 1 Cor 2[1–5] of his state of mind at this time—'in weakness and in fear and in much trembling'. He was alone; he faced, in Corinth, a city of notorious immorality; he was doubtful about the methods he had used in his approach to the Athenian philosophers; he was anxious about the state of the Macedonian churches, especially Thessalonica. At Corinth he met Aquila and Priscilla and settled down to work in their workshop, with synagogue evangelism on Saturdays. Until—at Acts 18[5]—Silas and Timothy join him from Macedonia.

Once again we are able to supplement Luke's brief account from Paul's own words. From 3[1-5] it is clear that Timothy, urgently summoned by Paul to Athens, had come there and then been sent back to Thessalonica, to help the Thessalonians and to bring news of their condition. (Luke does not tell us this, but we must not expect *Acts* to tell us everything.) Then in 3[6-10] Paul shares his intense relief from tension at the arrival of Timothy and the good news he brought from Thessalonica. He pours out his thankfulness in a letter, and deals with the Thessalonian problems which Timothy had reported. This then is *1 Thessalonians*, the letter with which we must grapple. We must try, with the Spirit's help, to find out what God said through Paul to that church so long ago; and then what He says through this letter to His Church today.

Thessalonians and the Preacher

How to Begin

WE are those into whose hands God has put this part of His word, those whom He sends out to proclaim, teach and show forth its message in this modern world. This is a very difficult task; indeed an utterly impossible task, apart from faith and prayer. We must begin then, with *prayer*—for ears to hear what the Spirit is saying to the churches; for minds to understand these Epistles and this modern world; and, so that our message may be understood, 'words found for us not by our human wisdom but by the Spirit'. Above all, we must pray for *faith*, faith that God really does intend to speak through these Epistles today. This needs a good deal of faith! They are no happy hunting ground for preachers. At first sight, most of the mighty themes of the gospel appear to be lacking in them, apart from the 'Second Coming', so unpalatable to modern ears, and apparently so irrelevant. Much of them seems to be taken up with the details of Church life in a bygone age, personal relationships between people long ago, and difficult answers to questions we do not ask. But if we study the Epistles in depth and with imagination, we shall find that these preliminary judgements need revision. The Epistles are not so lacking in the mighty themes of the gospel after all! We have found it necessary, in addition to the commentary, to direct the preacher to nineteen themes for preaching, themes which cover the whole sweep of the faith. Not only do we have death, judgement, Antichrist and the Parousia, but the Holy Trinity, Father, Son and Holy Spirit, Satan, the Church, the preacher and the word of God; and a series of themes concerning the Christian life—election, holiness, suffering, prayer, edification, work, discipline. And this is by no means the end of the matter. 'The Lord hath yet more light and truth to break forth from His holy word.' If we go further still, we shall find that the very things which, at first sight, seemed to disqualify these Epistles for relevance to life today, are

in fact among the prime needs of the modern Church and
the modern world. There is much, it is true, about problems
and personal relationships of a bygone age. But if we live
ourselves into the Epistles we can return to today with
a better understanding of the need to deal, in our preaching,
with *real problems*, and to give the answers, not only in words,
but in restored personal relationships. And the Second
Coming, even if it *is* unpalatable, is far from irrelevant. Paul
described the world in which *we* preach when he spoke of 'the
rest which have no hope'. To a world which tries to build
upon 'the firm foundation of unyielding despair' we must
proclaim, in contemporary terms, the Christian *hope*, and
demonstrate, in word, action and life, that we can 'give answer
to every man that asketh a reason concerning the hope that is
in us'.

Commentary

1^1: Greeting

'THE three members of the Gospel Band, to those Thessalonians whom God, in Christ, has made His people, grace to you and peace.'

An ancient letter began with the formula 'A to B greeting'. We may compare 'Claudias Lysias unto the most excellent governor Felix, greeting' (Greek *chairein*), in Acts 23^{26} (cf. Jas 1^1). Paul takes this epistolary formula and baptizes it into Christ. The three who had brought the gospel to Thessalonica stand as the senders. The plural is used throughout (apart from 2^{18}, 3^5, 5^{27}). But we need not suppose that the letter is a piece of committee-drafting (see comment on 3^1). *Paul* writes, but from the fellowship of the preachers.

Paul—chief Pharisee (Gal 1^{13-14}), apprehended by Christ (Phil 3^{12}), and made apostle to the Gentiles. By this act of Christ he was made a living embodiment of 'grace' (1 Cor 15^{10}), a perpetual reminder to the Church that God is a 'God of wonders'. But here he is not 'Paul the apostle', but 'Paul the man'. In this letter, and the other letter to a beloved Macedonian church (Phil 1^1), he is simply 'Paul'. And so, no doubt, he would always have chosen to write. But when doubts were cast on the reality of Christ's sending, he was compelled to write as 'Paul, called to be an apostle of Jesus Christ through the will of God' (1 Cor 1^1; cf. Gal 1^1).

Silvanus (2 Cor 1^{19}, 1 Pet 5^{12}) is the same as the Silas of Acts 15–18. We meet him first at Jerusalem at the Apostolic Council as a 'chief man among the brethren' (Acts 15^{22}), and so, presumably, a Christian of the very first generation. With Judas Barsabbas he was sent to Antioch, to prove by his presence and his words that there was no split between Paul and the mother church. He was a Jew, a prophet (Acts 15^{32}) and a Roman citizen (Acts 16^{37}). He worked and suffered with Paul in Philippi, Thessalonica and Corinth. After that we hear no

more of him until he turns up again in connection with Peter
in 1 Pet 5^{12}. E. G. Selwyn thinks there is sufficient similarity
between the language of *1 Peter* and the Thessalonian letters to
make it probable that Silvanus had a large part in the writing
of both letters. But the evidence is slight.

Timothy—the most frequently mentioned of all Paul's helpers.
When, at the beginning of the second missionary journey,
having exchanged Silas for Barnabas and being still in need of
someone to replace John Mark, Paul came to Lystra, he took
note of the good reports, not only from Lystra but also from
Iconium, about Timothy, who must have been converted on
Paul's first journey (1 Cor 4^{17}). Just the man for the job!
Except that his mother, in spite of the piety and Bible-reading
she had received from *her* mother (2 Tim 1^5, 3^{15}) had married a
Gentile and neglected to arrange for her son's circumcision.
In his eagerness to have Timothy's services, Paul pushed his
principle of behaving as a Jew to Jews (1 Cor 9^{20}) to the limit,
and circumcised him. From then on he was Paul's loyal
colleague. 1 Cor 16^{10} makes us think that he was nervous;
Phil 2^{22} and 1 Tim 4^{12} that he was young. But Paul valued him
very highly, as we see not only from 3$^{1-5}$, but from 1 Cor 4^{17},
16^{10}, Rom 16^{21}, Phil 2$^{20-2}$ (see *KG*, 100). Although he may not
have played a very prominent part in the Thessalonian mission,
he had recently conducted his first independent assignment with
marked success (see comment on 3$^{1-10}$).

So the 'gospel band'—apostle, exhorter (Acts 15^{32}) and
'young man'—address the '*church of the Thessalonians in God
the Father and the Lord Jesus Christ*'.

'*church*'. The Greek word (*ecclesia*) would be well known in
the Greek city of Thessalonica. There it would mean (as in
Acts 19$^{32-8, 40}$) the assembly of the citizens called together to
conduct the affairs of the city. But, since the Pauline mission,
there had come to be another *ecclesia* in Thessalonica. For
this new *ecclesia* we must go to the OT, where the two Hebrew
equivalents mean the people of God, Israel, constituted by His
choice and call. Radically reformed and made new by the act
of God in Christ, the People of God was to be found in
such a place as Thessalonica—the '*ecclesia* in God and
Christ'. Paul uses this great phrase here and in the second

epistle (1¹)—and then drops it. The second half, 'in Christ,' he develops into one of his most characteristic expressions.

'*in God*' comes again in 2²; then not till Col 3³, Eph 3⁹. What does the phrase mean here? It used to be thought that the metaphor was from an environment—like a fish in water, or man in his atmosphere. The Christian similarly lives, moves and has his being '*in God*' and Christ. But Paul did not think of God and Christ as air and water in this way. 'In Christ' is much more likely to be contrasted with 'in the world' (Eph 2¹²) or 'in Adam' (1 Cor 15²²). Then the idea is of a close-knit community or 'solidarity'. The whole human race is a community 'in the world'; a solidarity 'in Adam'. And, as a contagious disease might affect a whole family, the Bible thinks of the whole human race as affected by sin, and so deprived of true light and life. But because of the act of God in Christ, believers have been brought into a new community—the 'body of Christ', where they are related to Christ and so to one another in a radically new way. So the new 'people of God' is 'in Christ', and so in (a new relationship to) God. God is 'Father'—revealed as such in Christ, through whom believers become His adopted children (Rom 8¹⁵).

'*Jesus*', a man, was '*Christ*', the Messiah in whom all God's promises were fulfilled. That same '*Jesus Christ*' was made '*Lord*' (Acts 2³⁶, Phil 2¹¹), the object of Christian allegiance and worship.

Now comes the greeting—'grace' and 'peace'. The Greek greeting, as we noted, was *chairein;* the Jews' was *shalom* (compare the 'salaam' of Eastern countries), meaning peace. Paul takes the formula *chairein* and changes it to the similar word *charis*, '*grace*'; he translates *shalom* into '*peace*'. Grace is what happened when God commended His love towards us in that while we were yet sinners, Christ died for us (Rom 5⁸). It is God's love showered decisively on the undeserving (see *KG* 14, *HKM* 80, 91 f). Peace is the gift which came and comes to us through grace-restored relationships with God, and so with His world and with other people (see *KG* 15, *HKM* 9).

Note 1: *God, Father and Son*

A preacher in the atomic age! Is he a pathetic anachronism? Or a man with the most challenging, relevant and dangerous

of all possible tasks? This is certainly a time of challenge—the
post-Christendom age, when the Church can count on no
entrenched privileges; the age of secularization, which speaks
a new language, into which the gospel must be translated; the
Bultmann, Tillich, Robinson, van Buren age, when ancient
shibboleths and time-honoured formulae have gone into the
melting-pot, and the most fundamental concepts of the gospel
must be courageously re-thought. The preacher in the atomic
age is one who takes up the challenge, in the faith that the
eternal gospel, reinterpreted without loss and declared in contemporary terms, is the only thing which can meet the urgent
needs of the present age. This taking up of the challenge is a
dangerous business. We stand on a precarious razor-edge. On
the one side yawns the chasm of sterility—refusal really to face
the challenge; preaching instead in meaningless words to dwind-
ling congregations of irrelevant saints. But the chasm on the
other side is at least equally terrifying—the substitution of a
new message for the old; preaching what this age would like
to hear and calling it the gospel. If we are to stand on the
razor-edge, stand firm and then walk forward, we need three
things—understanding of the Bible message; courage to take
up all categories available to express that message; and wisdom
to know which categories illuminate, and which betray, the
gospel.

We take up in this *Note* the preaching of God the Father and
God the Son, and in *Note* 16 continue with a consideration of
God the Holy Spirit and God the Holy Trinity.

A. The message of *Thessalonians* about God the Father is
contained in three great titles.

(*1*) He is 'the living and true God' (1⁹, *NEB*). He is over
against idols and 'all that is called God' (2 Thess 2⁴). His life
is revealed in His activity in the history of the world He has
made. He has qualities, especially *truth*. He is true to Himself
and to His people, reliable, trustworthy.

(*2*) He is '*Father*' (1¹) and '*our Father*' (1³, 3¹¹, 3¹³, 2 Thess
1¹, 2¹⁶). This title describes the authority and love of the
Creator, the '*Father of our Lord Jesus Christ*', through whom
He adopts us into His family, the Church.

(*3*) He is '*God of peace*' (5²³). This peace (no negative
absence of strife but the sum of all blessedness) God *has*, *gave*
and *gives*.

We ought to note other passages in these Epistles which fill out the picture. There are *verbs* which set forth the action of the living God. There is action in the past: He loved, He gave (2 Thess 2¹⁶), He appointed (5⁹), He chose (2 Thess 2¹³), He raised from the dead (1¹⁰), He approved (2⁴). There is action in the present: He gives (4⁸), He calls (5²⁴). There is action in the future: He will bring (4¹⁴). Here is action which had a beginning (2 Thess 2¹³), a decisive centre (1¹⁰), and will have an End. The *nouns* combined with the word 'God' continue the story. We read of His kingdom and glory (2¹²), His gospel and word (2², 2¹³), His churches and fellow-workers (2¹⁴, 3²), His will for His people (4³).

This is the message which we, as preachers, have to translate into the language of the atomic age. In so far as our work is a matter of translation, we may expect to get help from those who are engaged in the translating or re-translating of biblical texts into the spoken languages of the world today. Anyone who has had experience of this work would say at least four things:

(*i*) It is essential to know the language into which the translation is to be made. This knowledge comes not only from grammar books and lexicons, but from prolonged contact with those who actually speak the language now.

(*ii*) It is equally necessary to know the biblical language at depth, i.e. to know, not the literal translation of the original words, but their essential meaning. Good translation is not literal translation, but it *is* a reproduction of the meaning of the original. And the Bible text must be allowed to have the last word. How often a fine-sounding, intelligible phrase has to be rejected because it does not mean what the text means.

(*iii*) The languages are often deficient in words required to express biblical concepts. In that case translators must choose the least unsuitable words and fill them with new meaning. But sometimes they are driven to let the Bible modify the language of translation by introducing new words!

(*iv*) All translators know that, however carefully and laboriously they do their work, the Bible cannot be made intelligible by words alone. Behind the written and spoken word there must be the Church, translating the text into life.

These four 'translation truths' will help us in our preaching:

(*i*) We all know something of atomic age language. It is the language of an age of science and technology which tends to find meaning only in statements capable of scientific verification. But do we know the language well enough? Have we learnt too much of it from books? Preaching about God cannot be done in the ghetto. The whole Church—parsons, lay preachers, laity in general—must come out of the ghetto and *by meeting people* become really proficient in their language. Perhaps lay preachers, with more opportunities of contact than parsons, but with similar responsibilities for expression, have a key part to play here.

(*ii*) Current translators have rightly revolted against the continued use of outmoded language. As omnicompetent science increasingly takes over the management of the world, God tends to be pushed further and further away from the centre of life towards the gaps and the edges. Today the word 'God' means for many 'Someone up there', 'Someone out there', 'Someone *there*'. Retranslation is urgently needed to show that God is *here*, in the depth, in the midst of whatever is being taken seriously. So new translators suggest such translations as 'Ground of our being', 'the Beyond in the midst'. Are such phrases adequate translations of what the Bible really *means*? If we take *Thessalonians* as an example of what we have to translate, it is very doubtful whether they are adequate. We have to 'get across' that God is 'living and true', that He is 'Father', that He is 'God of peace'. We cannot do this without the use of two categories—*personality* and *activity in history*. It is true that God is not there but here, very much in the midst. But He is the midst as the Other, who created and loves us, and to whom we are responsible. And He is in the midst as One who acted in Christ, who is active now, and who will act in the future. To remove these two categories is to be 'untrue to the text'. Words like 'the Ground' and 'the Beyond' are insufficiently personal and dynamic. It looks as if the work of translation is not yet complete.

(*iii*) *No* essentially scientific language is adequate to express personal realities, any more than a two-dimensional map of the world can tell the whole truth about the reality it seeks to portray. We must let the gospel break through in judgement and create new meaning in a language or a philosophy completely tied to scientific verification.

(*iv*) But however much we struggle with *words*, the world will only believe when the words are translated into action. No preaching which does not aim, first and foremost, for this, can be adequate to the needs of today.

Thy wonders wrought already
Require our ceaseless praises;
But show Thy power,
And myriads more
Endow with heavenly graces.
But fill our earth with glory,
And, known by every nation,
God of all grace
Receive the praise
Of all Thy new creation. (*MHB* 251)

B. What is the message of these epistles about the Lord Jesus Christ? Let us take each of these words separately.

(*1*) There is not much about the *life* of the *Jesus* of history. The main stress is on the great historical salvation-events; the crucifixion (2¹⁵), that 'death for us' (5¹⁰, 4¹⁴), and the resurrection (1¹⁰, 4¹⁴). But in 1⁶ suffering Christians are said to be imitators of their suffering Lord. And twice Paul makes an especially significant use of the name Jesus. In 1¹⁰ it is *Jesus* (the *man*) who is our Saviour; in 4¹⁴ it is *Jesus* who died and rose again, who will bring those who 'died through Him'.

(*2*) Such passages as 5⁹, 5¹⁸, 2 Thess 2¹⁴ show what Paul meant by the word *Christ*. Through what happened in the life, death and resurrection of Jesus, God brought to historical fulfilment His 'appointment', 'will', 'choice'. Because of these events, believers have ceased to be 'in Adam', and have come to be 'in Christ' (see *VT* 43; *KG* 47, 79; *GPL*, *Note* 10, p. 48). And this state of being 'in Christ' is something which the fact of physical death does not alter (4¹⁶).

(*3*) But the Jesus Christ we meet in *Thessalonians* is above all '*the Lord*'. Jesus, the man who lived and died; Jesus Christ, whose life, death and resurrection were the context of God's decisive act in the midst of history; He is Jesus Christ our *Lord*, possessor of 'the name which is above every name' and 'all authority in heaven and earth', whose servants, or slaves, we are. Relationships to the Lord span the whole life of believers. They 'stand in the Lord' (3⁸); Paul begs, exhorts and commands 'in the Lord' (4¹); local leaders lead 'in the Lord' (5¹²). But the special stress in these letters is on waiting for the Coming Lord (1¹⁰). On the day of the Lord, the Lord Himself will come for judgement and salvation. The Lord, through whom the

history of God's world had a decisive centre, will bring it to a
victorious end.

Each generation must answer the question, 'But who say ye
that I am?' (Mk 8^{29}). The apostles proclaimed 'God hath made
him both Lord and Christ, this Jesus'. The later Church
interpreted Him as 'truly man and truly God'. There is no
escape for the preacher of today from the reassessment and
re-interpretation of Jesus which is everywhere demanded. The
'New Theology' has turned to a new study of Jesus the man,
as He appears in the Synoptic Gospels. And surely this is the
right place to begin. The only trouble is that they turn to the
NT after having demolished 'God out there' in such a way as
to rule out the possibility that traditional formulations of the
doctrine of the Incarnation might enshrine truth capable of
reinterpretation for today. This is very unscientific! We must
simply 'consider Jesus'. Perhaps the key is to be found where
Dr D. M. Baillie found it in *God was in Christ*—in what he
calls 'the central paradox'. As we 'consider Jesus' we cannot
fail to be struck by the fact that, though He makes great claims,
He claims nothing for Himself, but ascribes all glory to God
(cf. e.g. Mk 10^{17} and Jn 5^{19}; see *CLM*, *OEE*). Baillie interprets
this fact as the supreme example of the central paradox—the
paradox of grace. This is the paradox expressed by Paul in
1 Cor 15^{10}—'I laboured more abundantly that they all; yet not
I but the grace of God . . . ' The true Christian is one who
ascribes all that is good in him to God alone, to God's act and
initiative. The supreme goodness of Jesus is ascribed by Him
to the initiative of God. The way is open for a restatement of
Jesus as truly man and truly God. The New Theology also
fastens on one side of the paradox. Jesus claimed nothing for
Himself. He was 'the man for others', the one in whom love
had completely taken over. Because He was totally emptied
of self, He is a 'window into God at work'. But if we study the
Gospels without new theological prejudices we shall surely
judge that there are two things we cannot take away from the
Jesus of the Gospels. One is His personal communion with
the Father; He was 'the man for others' because He was 'the
man for God'. The other is the conviction that His life and
death are the fulfilling of God's purpose; 'howbeit not what I
will, but what thou wilt'. But the crucial matter is the Resurrection. The New Theology is embarrassed by it, and tends
to interpret it as a subjective and ultimately inexplicable

experience of the disciples. But is Jesus alive now or not? If He is not, then surely Paul is right and 'we are of all men most pitiable'. If He is, then surely we can trust Him to give us, through the Spirit, the words to make clear what it means that He is Christ and Lord. Provided, of course, that we ourselves show forth, as individuals and as a community, what the acceptance of His Lordship means, in action and life. What we need is the commitment and the fervour of

> *Happy, if with my latest breath*
> *I might but gasp His name;*
> *Preach Him to all, and cry in death:*
> *Behold, behold the Lamb! (MHB 92)*

And oh for a new Charles Wesley, to set the atomic age singing the gospel!

(A) 1²–3¹³: Praise God! For the Preaching of the Gospel in Thessalonica, its reception and its Fruit

(1) 1²–2¹⁶: How They Brought the Good News

(a) 1²⁻¹⁰: *A Model Church*

Summary: *Three things which make a model church—(i) true conversion; (ii) the translation of theological words like 'faith', 'hope' and 'love' into Christian living; (iii) evangelism*

In the ancient letter-formula, the greeting was followed by a thanksgiving which was often a mere formality. How Paul makes dead bones live! From now till 2¹⁴ he pours out his heartfelt thanksgiving to God for what the Holy Spirit has done to the preachers and through the preachers in Thessalonica.

1². *RV* takes the adverb *'without ceasing'* with *'remembering'*; *RSV* and *NEB* with *'making mention'*. The latter is preferable —compare Rom 1⁹. The gospel band give thanks always,

make mention without ceasing. Their work was based on
frequent and regular prayer (as all fruitful preaching must be).
And no prayer was without thanksgiving to God for all the
Thessalonian Christians (even though, as we shall see, many of
them were far from perfect). Paul's thought of individuals is
dominated by his thought of the community of the people of
God.

1³. The food for thanksgiving was their vivid memory of the
'*work of faith and labour of love and patience of hope*'. Here we
have the famous trio of 1 Cor 13¹³, a favourite with Paul (see
5⁸, Rom 5²⁻⁵, Gal 5⁵⁻⁶, Col 1⁴⁻⁵). But it is not confined to
Paul (see Heb 6¹⁰⁻¹², *RW*; 1 Pet 1²¹⁻²) and may be a beloved
commonplace of primitive Christianity. In 1 Cor 13¹³, we have
the order faith, hope, love; here faith, love, hope—which is
more logical. Faith points back from the present to the past,
to that crisis of meeting with Christ where relationships of
trust were established; love confesses the present receiving of
the gifts of the Spirit which faith made possible; hope points
from the present to the future as confident expectation of His
coming victory. But for the Thessalonians 'faith', 'love' and
'hope' were not merely interesting theological words; they had
been translated into *life*. Their *faith* was 'faith working' (Gal
5⁶; cf. *KG* 62), because it was a relation of trustful obedience
and obedient trust in Christ. Before the controversy which had
to thrust faith and works apart, how artlessly Paul shows the
true relation between them, seen in Thessalonian lives! *Love*
involved '*labour*'—hard, sweating toil for those who were
loved. And *hope* was the hope which showed itself in patience
—not a mere passive enduring, but a courageous, victorious
grappling with all the afflictions which seemed to contradict
the hope (see *HKM* 10). The sentence is really complete with
the word '*hope*'. But Paul finds it hard to achieve a full stop!
He adds two phrases—literally '*of our Lord Jesus Christ*' and
'*before our God and Father*'. *RSV* and *NEB* take the latter
with '*remembering*'—remembering before God. But the words
are too far apart for this. Some connect both phrases with
'*hope*' alone—hope in Christ's victory which will bring the
world before God. But it is best to think that Paul connects
Christ and God thus intimately with all the preceding words.
For faith and love, no less than hope, are 'of *our Lord Jesus
Christ*'; the whole Christian life '*before God*'.

1⁴. Mention of the Thessalonians brings the memory of 'what God had wrought'. '. . . *brethren*'—a word of intimate Christian fellowship, found no less than 21 times in these letters. Let us not forget that Paul was a Pharisee and the '*brethren*' Gentiles. Such wonders love can do! But the fundamental reality is *God's* love. The Thessalonian believers are '*beloved of God*'—and the Greek tense is 'perfect with effects remaining', i.e. God has showered His love upon them *and loves them still*. What Paul and his companions know from their prayers is the *election* of the Thessalonians. As God chose a people in the OT, so He has chosen the Thessalonians now. This means that their faith rests primarily not on their choice, but on God's (cf. Jn 15¹⁵)—God who chooses not from man's goodness, but from His grace; not for privilege, but for responsibility. He chooses people to work for Him and for others. On '*election*' see *Note 15*, p. 98.

1⁵. As Denney says, 'the doctrine of election has often been taught as if the one thing that could never be known about anybody was whether he was or was not elect'. But Paul *knows* that the Thessalonians are elect, and that by three signs (translating the beginning of the verse with *RSV* as 'for our gospel . . .').

(*a*) by what God did when the gospel was preached to the Thessalonians. Paul calls it '*our gospel*'—the gospel with which he was 'approved of God to be entrusted' (**2⁴**)—the good news of God's mighty acts in Christ. Frail men opened their mouths and spoke words. But God took those words and charged them with the power of the Holy Spirit, creating absolute conviction in the preachers, which communicated itself to the hearers.

(*b*) by what God did in the lives of the preachers. The Thessalonians knew well what manner of men the preachers were— how their gospel was not only word, or even power, but life— and all (whatever might be said to the contrary) for the sake of the hearers.

1⁶. (*c*) by what God did in the lives of the hearers, who '*became imitators of us, and of the Lord*'. Sometimes a great gulf is fixed between Pauline Christianity and the Synoptic Gospels

—but here it is the authentic 'Follow me', especially of Mk 8³⁴ (see *CLM* 65). The believers were turned towards the Lord in His earthly suffering and humiliation. But first the preachers followed Him themselves (1 Cor 11¹). The Thessalonians '*received the word*' (remarkable enough in itself, considering that it was a word of a crucified carpenter—a stumbling-block to Jews and folly to Greeks). But more than that, they received the affliction which accompanied the word, with the joy inspired by the Holy Spirit. And joy in affliction is the authentic sign of the action of God in the soul (see *HKM* 23; *KG* 85, 113).

1⁷. Paul, the Roman citizen, thinks province-wise, Macedonia and Achaia forming between them the whole of Greece. Here and there were little groups of believers. But the Thessalonians, because they had imitated the Lord, were themselves a '*model*' (*NEB*) to them all. To no other church does Paul apply this word.

1⁸. The Thessalonians are a model church, for from them '*the word of the Lord*' (a phrase found only here and in 2 Thess 3¹ for the more usual 'word of God') has '*sounded forth*' (rung out, *NEB*). The word is found only here; it refers to some loud sound, like thunder or a trumpet, which cannot fail to be heard. Thessalonica was strategically placed for evangelism, on the road-sea communications system of a travelling age; and no doubt whenever Thessalonian believers travelled they witnessed. But this is not Paul's main meaning. The Thessalonian mission had become the equivalent of front-page news. Far beyond the borders of Greece ('*in every place*', says Paul, with pardonable 'pride'), people had heard of the Thessalonians putting their faith in God. So Paul did not need to tell people about Thessalonica; he found they already knew! Some real experience must lie behind this. News of the Christian revolution in Thessalonica (Acts 17⁶) would speedily have gone *to* Rome. Perhaps when Paul reached Corinth he found that Priscilla and Aquila, recently come *from* Rome (Acts 18²), had already heard—

1⁹⁻¹⁰—how the preachers had been received, and the extraordinary things that had happened as a result of their visit. In these verses we can see the sort of preaching Paul had used at Thessalonica, and find it to be very much like the preaching at

Lystra (Acts 14$^{15-17}$) and Athens (Acts 17$^{24-31}$).   There was

1. A prophetic protest against idolatry (cf. Isa 44$^{9-20}$).   Idols, for the Bible, are unreal and lifeless, powerless in their multiplicity to provide man with any stable system of thought or morals, delivering him to the domination of self-centredness and evil (1 Cor 10$^{19-22}$). See *GPL* 123–4.

2. A proclamation of God the living and the true, who is all that the idols are not; one where they are many, living where they are dead, real where they are false—God the self-consistent, the active, working out His purpose in His world.

3. A proclamation of the Son of God who has become man (Jesus), died, been raised again from the dead by God's decisive act, and exalted to God's right hand as living Lord.

4. A proclamation of Judgement to come.   God the living and the true is the Righteous and Holy One, part of whose love is *wrath*—an utterly righteous opposition to evil.   This wrath would soon culminate in the coming of the living Lord to judge and destroy all that is evil.   In the judgement man needs a Saviour, and that Saviour is the same Jesus.

Such was the gospel which had been proclaimed with such power.   In response to it, the Thessalonians had '*turned*' from idols to God the living and the true; had given themselves to His service, putting themselves entirely at His disposal for the working of His purposes, as slaves are at the disposal of their masters; and had entered a life of confident waiting for the final victory of the One who had been raised from the dead, aware of wrath to come, still more aware of the Saviour.

Much of Paul's gospel is implicit rather than explicit here— the turning to God involves faith and justification; the relation to Christ is present as well as future (a life 'in Christ'); the saving from wrath was accompanied by the atoning death.   But the main affirmations of the 'word of the Lord' are here in essentials—the coming into the world of the Son of God, His death and resurrection, His glorious, imminent coming, and the judgement of the quick and the dead.

N.B. For 1$^{9-10}$, see also *Note* 1.

Note 2: The Church

The church of the Thessalonians is put before us here as an '*ensample to all*' (*v.* 7).   We must certainly put it before our people, in challenge and encouragement!

C

A. First, 'church' as it appears in our Epistles. The word *ekklesia* occurs four times. Both Epistles are written to '*the church of the Thessalonians in God the (our) Father and the Lord Jesus Christ*' (1^1, 2 Thess 1^1). In 2^{14} we read that the Thessalonian brethren were imitators in suffering of '*the churches of God which are in Judaea in Christ Jesus*'; and in 2 Thess 1^4 that Paul gloried in them '*in the churches of God*'. Already, in these four brief verses, we have the heart of the matter, in two small prepositions. Churches are '*of* God' and '*in* God' (or '*in* Christ'). They are '*of* God' because they owe their origin to Him, belong to Him, exist for the fulfilment of His purposes. They are able to fulfil His purposes, in speech, action and life, because they are '*in* God' or '*in* Christ'. We have attempted to expound these phrases in the comment on 1^1. As we *preach* them, let us at all costs avoid the idea of a vague impersonal God-atmosphere, in which the individual Christian swims about like a goldfish in a bowl. Let us preach what God did in Christ to bring us from the world of broken relationships ('in Adam'), to the world of relationships restored (with God, our brethren and the world). But let us always preach this message as a challenge to the Church of today to show forth in its life what it means to be 'in Christ'.

We have found the gospel in two small prepositions! Here are some more. What about a sermon, which almost makes itself, on the prepositions joined with the word 'God' in these Epistles? A life turned *towards* God (1^9); lived *before* God (1^3, 3^9, 3^{13}); rooted *in* God (1^8, 2^2); receiving *from* God (2 Thess 1^2).

B. The whole passage (1^{2-10}) cries out to be taken as a text. Taken as a whole it shows the three relationships involved in the idea of the Church—(*a*) a new relationship to God, through His initiative and man's response, (*b*) the new relationship of Christian fellowship, cutting across all man-made barriers, because it is love, not of those *we* have chosen, but those whom He has effectually called, and (*c*) a new relationship to the world, for God's people are not only called out of the world, but back into the world, to work for Him. Such a sermon might start with

(*a*) *vv.* 9–10. What does it mean today (*i*) to turn from idols (*ii*) to God the living and true, so as to spend the life He has given in His service (*iii*) a service related to Jesus as living Saviour ('*raised from the dead*') (*iv*) in confident Christian hope of His coming victory (there will be much more about this as the letter proceeds).

(*b*) *vv.* 3–6. The new relationship of Christian fellowship works out in faith, love and hope shown forth in action; and the human impossibility ('*in the Holy Ghost*') of joy in affliction. Other passages in these Epistles reveal that this model church lacked much (3¹⁰). There are the disorderly, the faint-hearted and the weak (5¹⁴). This church is a model, not because of the perfection of its individual members, but because, with all its imperfections, it is set in prayer under the sign and challenge of perfection (3¹³, 5²³), and each is given the responsibility for every other in consolation and building up (4¹⁸, 5¹¹).

(*c*) *v.* 8. The word has sounded forth from the model church. As we saw in the commentary, it sounded forth not only in word but in action and life. And so, in the rest of the Epistle, Paul prays that their hearts may be stablished 'in every good word and work' (2 Thess 2¹⁷), including, of course, the word of witness. But behind this good word is a love which follows '*after that which is good*' . . . '*toward all*' (5¹⁵), a life which walks '*honestly toward them that are without*' (4¹²).

C. We take a brief opportunity here to show how inexhaustible the Bible is, and how inadequate such notes as these are bound to be. This one passage teems with sermons urgently needed these days. We mention only four, on four great theological words.

There is *faith* (*v.* 3)—faith as the human response to that utterly undeserved gift which is 'grace'; faith as personal relationship, faith in Christ; the essential connection of faith with works, 'faith working through love' (Gal 5⁶).

Then *love* (*v.* 3). Do our congregations really understand the distinction between God's '*agape*' and human '*eros*'? The showing forth of '*agape*' in the Cross (Rom 5⁸); the obligation (Jn 13³⁴) and possibility (Rom 5⁵) of the showing forth of '*agape*' by the Church now (see *VT* 37 f; *GPL, Notes* 9, 11, 16).

Then *conversion* (*v.* 9)—its threefold nature: turning to God, to one another, to the world.

Then *wrath*, an almost unintelligible word these days. But if God is holy love, He must oppose evil. Our people must understand Rom 1¹⁸⁻³², the revelation of wrath in the *consequences* of sin (see *VT* 24; *HKM* 47). What does 'fleeing from the wrath to come' mean today but the life of Christian *service*?

D. The Church in these Epistles, then, is (*i*) the place where there is turning from idols to God, (*ii*) the place where theological language is translated into Christian living, (*iii*) the place from which the word of the Lord sounds forth. Dynamic preaching along these lines will soon touch the main points at which the Spirit challenges the Church today.

(*1*) *The Church as a missionary body.* Christendom is dead. Not only on 'the mission field' but everywhere, the Church is the Remnant, scattered by God for mission. It is only the Church when it turns from idols to God, for service and evangelism, as 'the Church for others'.

(*2*) *Church Union.* If churches are societies we have formed for our own spiritual satisfaction, mergers can wait until we are ready . But we are called to proclaim that churches are 'in Christ' and 'of God'. Such preaching demands also consideration of how the truth behind 'in Christ' can be shown forth, and the truth behind 'of God' can be put into effective action. Both lines of thought lead directly to the divisions of the Church as an obscuring of the reality of our being 'in Christ', and a hindrance to a concerted effort to do His will.

(*3*) *The missionary structure of the congregation.* Once we grasp that the Church exists for mission, we must be ready for a bold stripping down of self-regarding structures, and an ever bolder planning for new ventures of infiltration and involvement in the life of this secularized age.

> *Head of Thy Church, whose Spirit fills*
> *And flows through every faithful soul,*
> *Unites in mystic love, and seals*
> *Them one, and sanctifies the whole:*
>
> *O for Thy truth and mercy's sake*
> *The purchase of Thy passion claim!*
> *Thine heritage, the nations, take,*
> *And cause the world to know Thy name.*
>
> (*MBH* 814)

(b) 2$^{1-12}$: *Model Preachers*

Summary: *Three things which make model preachers—(i) God's call, accepted whole-heartedly, with all the suffering involved; (ii) a life in agreement with the message preached;*

(*iii*) *love for people, as tender as a mother's love, as strong
as a father's.*

The background of this passage is a whole host of the Hyde
Park orators of that day. Neil puts the situation well. 'Holy
men of all creeds and countries, popular philosophers, magic-
ians, astrologers, crack-pots and cranks; the sincere and the
spurious, the righteous and the rogue, swindlers and saints,
jostled and clamoured for the attention of the credulous and
the sceptical' (*Moffatt Commentary*, 36). When Paul and his
companions came to preach in Thessalonica, they had to
compete with other wandering preachers, many of them apt
targets for the charges of error, uncleanness, guile, flattery,
covetousness and glory-seeking of which this passage speaks.
Paul gives thanks to God that his work is clear of all these
charges. Are we to suppose that he is replying to actual charges
actually made? Most commentators think that he is—that
Timothy brought news of Jewish slanders that Paul was 'no
better than the other rogues and swindlers'. The strange thing
is that, if this is mainly self-defence, it is so unimpassioned,
lacking the fire and heartbreak of the self-defence in *2
Corinthians* and the forthrightness of 2^{15-16}. Paul knew, of
course, that the Thessalonian Christians did not believe the
charges (3^6). But even so, he does not write as if his main aim
is self-defence. Some, e.g. Dibelius, have thought that no such
charges were made, but that Paul is simply recalling the Thessalonian preaching—part of which included, he thinks, a series
of disclaimers by Paul of motives which might be alleged
against other preachers. There may perhaps be something of
this kind behind *v.* 3. But it is hard to deny that some charges
had been made. What we have to remember is that in this
whole section Paul is thanking God for what He had done in
the preachers ($1^{5, 9}$, 2^{1-12}) and for what He had done in the
hearers (1^{6-10}, 2^{13-14}). We cannot exactly tell how much of
the passage is due to charges and how much to recollection.
But though there may have been charges, bitterness is swal-
lowed up in thankfulness. Against the background of attacks
and memories, Paul lets his light shine before men, that they
may glorify God.

2^1. 'They themselves report . . . about our entering in . . . to
you' (1^9). But the Thessalonian brethren themselves knew

about that '*entering in*'—that it was not '*vain*', devoid of content and result. It would have been vain if Paul had had no gospel, if the Thessalonians had not believed. But it was an entering in charged with the dynamite of the Holy Spirit.

2². One of the reasons for the power of his gospel was Paul's readiness to suffer for it. He had come, with his colleagues, from the 'injury and outrage' (*NEB*) they had suffered at Philippi—bodies bruised and wounded (Acts 16²²⁻³), hearts even more lacerated by the insult and 'loss of face' to which, as Roman citizens, they had been subjected (Acts 16³⁷⁻⁸). But they did not run away. They 'had courage in their God'—in their relationship to Him (see comment on **1¹**)—to declare the good news in much conflict. There has been much discussion about whether this conflict (the usage is from the games—the effort required for the wrestling match) was external or internal. Surely it was both. The conflict was Paul's side of the affliction (**1⁶**) which came to the Thessalonians.

2³. Bold in God, and full of power in the midst of suffering and opposition—what is to be said of such men and their exhortation (i.e. their preaching directed as an appeal to the decision of the hearers)? There are things it is *not*—not based on '*error*' (delusion); not inspired by '*uncleanness*' (impurity) (not merely impurity of motive, but sexual immorality, a very frequent concomitant of 'religion' in those days—one against which Paul will have to caution the Thessalonians in chapter 4); nor carried on in an atmosphere of '*guile*' (no propaganda methods barred, so long as they gain the hearers).

2⁴. No. No delusion, impurity or guile. For '*God which proveth*' (tests, judges) '*our hearts*' (our inmost personality) is the one by whom *we* have been tested and (having been found to be men whose pride has been shattered by grace) have been found worthy to be entrusted with the gospel. Men who have experienced such a shattering, and who still stand day by day before such a judgement, are men who have renounced delusion, impurity and guile—who speak not as men-pleasers (cf. 1 Kings 22¹³⁻¹⁴), but as men whose one aim is to please God the 'living and true'.

2⁵⁻⁶. Three more things from which the appeal of Paul had been free—flattering words (the Thessalonians, whose sins had been laid bare, knew *that* well enough); the use of the gospel as a smoke-screen to hide an underlying greed (*RSV, NEB*)—a ruthless selfishness which utterly ignores the rights of others (God who tests the heart knew *that*); seeking honour, glory, praise from men. That they had never done.

Though in fact they were apostles of Christ, i.e. sent by Christ as His envoys, with His authority. Consequently they might, as *NEB* well translates, have made their weight felt. This is the only occasion in these letters when Paul brings forward his calling as an apostle, and here he associates Silvanus and Timothy with him in Christ's sending. But when need arose, as it did in *Galatians* or *Corinthians*, Paul can defend with great vigour his claim to be an apostle of Christ in a very special sense, one of a limited number, including 'the twelve' who received a special commission from the Risen Christ (1 Cor 15^{1-11}). In this sense, Timothy is not an apostle. In our eagerness for the equality of ministries, we must not forget their diversity.

2^7 *'gentle'* (cf. 2 Tim 2^{24})—gentle as a nurse brooding over the children, caring for them, keeping them warm. The word *'her'* may be translated 'her own' (cf. 'his own', 2^{11})—i.e. Paul here thinks of a nursing mother caring for the children she has borne in her own womb, nursed at her own breast. The true pastor is mother (and, as we shall see, father) to believers.

2^8. A rare word expresses the depth of the pastor's mother-love—'with such yearning love' (*NEB*). But this love is no mere sentimentality, but rather a love ready to share the treasures of *'the gospel of God'*—and not only the gospel, but the *'psyche'* of the preacher. This word can mean life, but the verb (sharing something with somebody) is decisive against the meaning of giving *life* for the other. What is shared is the 'very self', the personality. The gospel is shared in no 'take it or leave it' way, but with the infinitely costly involvement of love, symbolized by the mother pouring out her very self for her child. The love of the preacher is such love as that.

2^9. The brethren will not have forgotten another thing which distinguished the Pauline mission from all others. Paul's father, wealthy though he may have been, followed good Rabbinic precept in teaching his son a trade—that of a tent-maker (or perhaps a leather-worker). And in an age when manual labour was despised, Paul toiled and drudged ('toiled and moiled' as Lightfoot translated, getting the alliteration) night and day—hard, unremitting toil, so as not to be a burden (though he had every right to be, 2^6). So he showed his love in action, as in word he proclaimed (like a herald announcing the news of the day) the good news of what God had done.

2^{10}. Not only their manual labour—their whole life was a matter for witness; witness by God and the congregation. They were blameless, whether judged by God (holily), or man (righteously), in their behaviour to those '*that believe*'. Faith cleaves the city into two parts. Unbelievers can persecute and condemn; believers can witness to what they have seen. God is witness, because it was by His grace and before His judgement that their life was lived.

2^{11}. Mother, labourer, pattern,—and now '*father*'. The preacher has become a pastor who deals with '*each one*' of his children, exhorting and urging when that was needed, comforting and encouraging, appealing with solemnity and urgency —as a father with his own children.

2^{12}. To what end? To a walk worthy of God. It is not enough to *turn to God*. Believers must '*walk*' (for so Paul often describes the Christian life—it is fatal to stand still!). How? '*worthily of God*' (the whole law of God contracted to a span— live the sort of life worthy of what God has done for you). God '*calleth*'. He called at the time of conversion, but that call is constantly renewed, and regulates the whole Christian life. He calls each one to His '*kingdom and glory*'. God is King. His kingship is rejected in this sinful world. But one day, the Jews believed, it would be revealed in glory. The Christian good news is that the kingdom of God was revealed in Christ, revealed yet hidden in the humiliation of the Cross. One day it will be revealed in glory in that same Christ's 'coming'. God invites the believer into the coming glorious revelation of the kingdom. He must put on the wedding garment of a life worthy of that call.

Note 3: The Preachers Themselves

This would be a grand passage to take at an Ordination; for here is the classic portrait of God's minister.

(*a*) It all begins with God, who tests their hearts, approves them, and with sublime condescension entrusts His gospel to them. The human response to such grace is the total dedication to Him of the powers of speech, for the speaking of His good news (four times stressed, in *vv.* 2, 4, 8 and 9) and not any 'word of man'; the constant receiving of His boldness (*v.* 2) and His judgement (*vv.* 4, 5, 10) in a confident assurance of the greatness of the apostolic calling; and a humility which can forego all apostolic rights (*v.* 6).

(*b*) But the response to God's call to preach is not only the surrender of the powers of speech, but of all the vital powers. God's preachers not only speak, but pour out their strength and energy for their hearers (*v.* 9). They submit their lives to the suffering and toil inseparable from their calling (*v.* 2). Conscious of the temptations which beset them (how necessary it is to recognize the terrible six—delusion, uncleanness, guile, flattery, greed and glory-seeking—in their modern dress!), they are by His grace 'blameless', whether judged by God's requirement of holiness, or the world's, of integrity (*v.* 10). Their life agrees with their message.

(*c*) In particular, the response to the call is a life of love. This is made possible by the 'love of God . . . shed abroad in our hearts by the Holy Ghost' (Rom 5⁵). When this is received, the result is so far beyond a human possibility that it can only be described as the combination of the infinitely tender love of a mother and the strong, authoritative love of the father (*vv.* 7, 8, 11, 12)—directed (here is the miracle), not to 'relatives and friends', but to all God's people, to enemies, to the whole world.

But is this passage concerned only with 'the ordained ministry'? To answer this question we must glance at *Ephesians*. The Christian ministry, we are told (Eph 4⁷⁻¹¹), is a gift to His Church of the Risen and Ascended Lord. The purpose of this gift is explained in Eph 4¹² (see *HKM* 111). But there are differences of interpretation. The *RV* translation makes three purposes—(*a*) for the perfecting of the saints, (*b*) unto the work of ministering, (*c*) unto the building up of the body of Christ. *RSV* agrees. But *NEB* translates as follows: 'to equip God's people for work in his service, to the building up of the body of Christ'. This *NEB* translation differs from *RV* and *RSV* by the omission of a single comma (sometimes referred to by advocates of lay training as 'the devil's comma'!).

But the illumination of the purpose of the ministry is immense. This translation reduces the purposes for which the ministry was given to *one*—the building up of the body of Christ; and this building up is done as those who are chosen by Christ and given to the Church as 'ministers' equip every member of the body for the work of ministering. 'The ministry', according to this, has no exclusive function. It is given so that *everyone* may minister. It is not our purpose here to ask if this translation of the Greek of Eph 4¹² is correct. But we must ask whether the view of the ministry which it sets forth is borne out by the teaching of the rest of our Epistles, to which we now turn again.

We have, first, the 'apostles of Christ' (2⁷). The word apostle (*one sent*) is used of Paul, Silvanus and Timothy. But, as we have seen, there is a difference in their sending. Paul himself claims to be among the number of those sent *directly*. He is 'an apostle, not from men, neither through man, but through Jesus Christ and God the Father' (Gal 1¹). This is elaborated in 1 Cor 15, where Paul claims that his vision of the Risen Christ on the Damascus road was the last of a series of encounters through which the Christ called and sent a limited number of apostles in the strictest sense of the word. Silvanus, chosen and sent by the whole Church to Antioch (Acts 15²²), was further chosen as his associate by Paul (Acts 15⁴⁰). Timothy was also chosen by Paul to take the place of the 'attendant', John Mark (Acts 16³, 13⁵). But all three are 'apostles', sent by Christ. Perhaps we may compare them to the Chairman of the District, the Local Preacher, the Youth Club Leader—all working for Christ in various ways, all sent by Him.

But now we have to anticipate for a moment and look at 5¹²⁻¹⁴. Here we have a 'local ministry'. Here again there is the same pattern of divine initiative and human response. The Holy Spirit divides 'to each one severally, even as he will' (1 Cor 12¹¹). This act of God is recognized and honoured by the Church (see Acts 14²³). The calling of these local ministers is briefly described in three ways:

(*a*) They are '*over you in the Lord*' ('your leaders', *NEB*). Here is a leadership which has its origin in God's call and not in any human craving for power, and which is to be exercised after the pattern of the Lord's words (Mk 10⁴²⁻⁵) and example (Jn 13³⁻¹¹).

(*b*) They '*labour*' ('work hard', *NEB*). Paul's word covers 'church work' and 'work in the world', making no distinctions. Ministers are to expect esteem and love from the congregation because of this hard work, and for no other reason (5¹³).

(c) 'admonishing' ('counselling', *NEB*). This word has a good deal of the 'telling of faults, plain and home' in it, and so would be possible only in an atmosphere where God's love in the leaders met God's love in the led (5¹³).

The Church is required to give heed to the authoritative preaching and teaching of the apostles, and wholeheartedly to accept God's provision of local leadership (5¹³). But it is emphatically not the case that apostles and leaders are to do all the work. The Church is to recognize (5¹²) that God requires some to admonish. But in 5¹⁴ all the brethren are told to admonish. In consolation (4¹⁸), upbuilding (5¹¹) and discipline (2 Thess 3⁶, ¹⁴⁻¹⁵) there are responsibilities for all. It looks as if the *NEB* translation of Eph 4¹² is justified, at least so far as doctrine goes!

So let us set down what we believe about 'ministry'—and preach it till we have it! Christ is, of course, Himself the Minister, who was among us 'as One who serves' (Lk 22²⁷). As Risen Lord He continues His ministry through the work of the Holy Spirit in His Church. Christ calls the whole Church, and every individual in it, to ministry—to witness and service in word, deed and life. The ministry of the whole Church is represented and made effective through the special ministry of some. But the special ministry is there so that the whole Church, turned to God in faith and to one another in fellowship, may be equipped and turned out to the world in service and witness.

> *Thy only glory let them seek;*
> *O let their hearts with love o'erflow!*
> *Let them believe, and therefore speak,*
> *And spread Thy mercy's praise below.* (*MHB* 791)

(c) 2¹³⁻¹⁶. *The Word of God in Salvation and Judgement*

Summary: *Thank God you were able to distinguish between the Word of God and the word of man! The proof that it is the Word of God you have received is your brave reaction to persecution (the lot of Christ's Church from the beginning). But the Word of God, which for you means salvation, means judgement for your persecutors.*

2¹³. '*For this cause we also*' (better—'we for our part') '*thank God without ceasing*'. The whole section, from **1²**, is thanksgiving for two things—(*a*) the preaching of the gospel, (*b*) its reception (cf. **1⁶, ⁹, ¹⁰**). Paul has said much about (*a*); he now says more about (*b*). It was a matter for constant thanksgiving that the Thessalonians were able to tell the difference between two forms of speech—'*the word of men*'—fallible mortals expressing their views, and '*the word of God*'—human speech used by God as the vehicle of His categorical imperative. The Thessalonians heard the gospel preached, '*received*' it and '*accepted*' it (welcomed it to their hearts) as what in reality it was—the word of God. That word '*worketh*' (because charged by God with His energy), is living and active (Heb 4¹²; *RW* 35 f), able (Acts 20³²) to 'accomplish that which He pleases' (Isa 55¹¹). But note that, in spite of all its power, the word of God does not burst through shut doors—it works in those who 'believe', in whose hearts the door of faith is open.

2¹⁴. The sign of the working of the word of God is not worldly prosperity; nor, first and foremost, feelings of peace and joy; but the brave bearing of *suffering*. Paul had already said **(1⁶)** that the converted Thessalonians modelled their actions on the apostles and the Lord by bearing affliction with joy. Not only the Lord (Mk 8³¹) and His apostles, but all His people *must* suffer. Paul takes as his example the mother church in Judaea (Palestine), of which Silvanus was a member. The Church, whether Jew or Gentile, has always had to bear persecution. Paul speaks here of the communities of God's people, gathered by His call, geographically in Judaea; essentially in Christ. The Thessalonians had suffered from their (Gentile) compatriots (though, as we see from Acts 17, the persecution was instigated by the Jews), as the Jewish Christians in Palestine had suffered from *theirs*.

2¹⁵. As he dictated the word '*Jews*', Paul was suddenly moved to the fiercest tirade against his compatriots we find anywhere in his letters (though we may compare Mt 23³¹⁻⁶ and Acts 7⁵¹⁻³). Like an OT prophet, he lays bare their sins and thunders judgement. But this is only one side of the coin. We must not forget the other—his appreciation of his Jewish heritage (Rom 9⁴⁻⁵), his great love for them (Rom 9²⁻⁴), his obstinate hope for them (Rom 11²⁶). But here he is all condemnation.

There are six charges. (*1*)—and most grievous of all—they killed the Lord Jesus, or, as the Greek strikingly puts it, they actually killed the (divine) Lord,—that is the man Jesus (cf. Mk 12$^{1-12}$, Acts 2^{23}, etc.). (*2*) In the past they killed the prophets (Mt 23$^{31, 34, 37}$, Lk 13^{34}, 1 Kings 19^{10}, 2 Chr 24$^{21-2}$, Jer 2^{30}, Neh 9^{26}). (*3*) More recently they have repeatedly driven out the apostles (as they had done at Philippi, Thessalonica, Beroea). (*4*) They make no effort to do what Paul considers the main aim of the good life (2^4, 4^1, Rom 8^8, 2 Cor 5^9),—to please God. (*5*) They are the enemies of their fellowmen (*NEB*). This verdict recalls a famous pagan judgement on the Jews—that of Tacitus, the Roman historian, who in his histories (5^5) writes, 'they regard the rest of mankind with all the hatred of enemies'. But they are called enemies by Paul for a reason which would never have occurred to Tacitus—

2^{16}. (*6*)—because they hinder the preaching of the gospel, aimed at the salvation of the Gentiles. God is love; but holy love. In the universe He has made, sin must have consequences both present and future. Man's chief need is salvation from sin. This salvation is proclaimed in the good news of what God did for man in Christ. Salvation is, properly speaking, future (e.g. Rom 5$^{9-10}$; *VT*); but by faith in Christ, a man may even now possess that justification and reconciliation which put him on the sure road to salvation. There is no other way of salvation. Therefore the Jews who, having failed to accept salvation themselves, try to deny it to others, are indeed the enemies of mankind.

What do these six charges against the Jews amount to?— they '*fill up their sins*'. This is an OT quotation (Gen 15^{16}, Dan 8^{23}) and refers to a Jewish metaphor of the Judge counting up the good and bad deeds of a people till they reach a certain maximum. Paul maintains that the Jews have filled up their sins 'always', i.e. that wherever you look—at their relation to the OT people, to Christ, to His Gentile mission—the opposition of the Jews to God has consistently been at the maximum, with devastating judgement held off only by the mercy of God (Rom 2^4).

Now follows a difficult phrase—'*the wrath is come upon them to the uttermost*' ('at last', *RSV*; 'for good and all', *NEB*). Some have thought that this must refer to the supreme historical proof of God's judgement of the Jews—i.e. the fall of

Jerusalem—and that this is therefore a subsequent interpolation. But there is no manuscript evidence for such an idea (and in any case such an interpolation would have been more explicit). We must make what we can of the text as it stands.

The '*wrath*' (cf. 1^{10}) is God's righteous opposition to evil, which will culminate in the Last Judgement, thought of as near. But that wrath which will be openly revealed in the Last Judgement, says Paul, already '*is come*'. Now this is his idea also in Rom 1^{18-32} (see *VT* 24 f), where the wrath against the Gentiles is seen, by the insight of the gospel, to have come already—in the Gentiles giving up of themselves to evil, which is also God's judicial giving of them up. Here the same thing is said of the Jews. Their hardness of heart and unbelief, shown in all six charges, especially the last, is *itself* the judgement of God, His wrath. The difficulty, as the variant translations show, is to get the exact shade of meaning of *eis telos*, '*to the uttermost*'. This phrase can mean 'finally' (Lk 18^5), 'to the end' (Acts 10^{22}) and also 'for ever' and 'completely'. We need to choose a meaning which does not entirely exclude the possibility of Rom 11^{26}. The opposition of the Jews to the gospel is God's judgement that such opposition must be deprived of the gospel. The only hope would be an initiative from the side of God Himself, a Damascus road experience for the Jewish race. Which is exactly what Paul hopes for in Rom 11^{26}.

Note 4: The Word of God and the Word of Man

When Paul preached at Thessalonica, what he spoke was 'the word of God', and his hearers were able to distinguish between this 'word of God' and 'the word of men'. What do these things mean for us today?

Muslims believe that, when Mohammed received the word of God which is the holy Quran, God spoke and dictated directly. Mohammed was the passive recipient; his own personality played no part in this event of revelation. In the Bible things are not so simple. Outwardly there was nothing to distinguish Paul's preaching from the speaking of other preachers. The voice was human, the tone was Paul's, his mind was consciously in control of the choice of words, the construction of sentences, the use of illustrations. And yet this fully human speech was being used by God to make Himself known, to open in the hearers the door to that free human decision which would make of the spoken words either salvation or judgement. Fully human speech; and yet the word of God. This is a mystery analogous to the mystery of the person of Christ. 'The word of men' does not mean 'words spoken by a man', but words whose content is purely human, words which give expression to human opinions, recommendations, intentions, wishes, hopes. The Bible has no faith in such a 'word of men'. James' strictures on the tongue (Jas 3) are not untypical of the biblical view. However excellent human speech or wisdom may be (1 Cor 2[1]), in the end it 'puffs up' and does not build up (1 Cor 4[19], 8[2]). In what ways ought we to expect human speech to become 'the word of God' these days? Is anything more than words involved in 'speaking' the word of God? How can we be sure that what we are saying *is* the word of God and not the word of men?

We begin with 'preaching', and ask what it essentially *is*. We must note the view of many scholars that what we think of as preaching today would not have been considered by the early Christians as preaching at all. 'In the New Testament,' says Richardson (*Theological Wordbook*, 171) 'preaching has nothing to do with the delivery of sermons to the converted'. Philibert, in *Christ's Preaching and Ours* (39) writes: 'The Sunday sermon is an illusory substitute for preaching. The Church which tolerates this situation might be compared with a farmer who stayed at home and sowed his seed in the drawing room rather than venture out into the fields.' The justification for such views as these is that, in the NT, the language used to express the idea of preaching is taken from the context of the broadcasting of news by a herald. Just as, in time of war, a herald might ride into a town and announce, 'Good news, we have won the victory!', so the apostles were sent from place to place to announce the good news that God, in Christ, had won the victory. But the herald was essentially itinerant. He never 'stayed put'. Once he had announced his news, he went on to announce it to others who had not heard it. So, it is argued, *that* is preaching and it is sheer misuse of language to apply the word to the addressing, week by week, of the same faithful few. At first sight, this view of preaching seems to go too far. What of all the 'nominal Christians', or the occasional pagans in our pews? Are not *all* our 'faithful few' sinners who need to hear the good news of the gospel again and again? But if we think more deeply we shall surely see the need to

return to this NT view of preaching. If it is true that the
Christendom era is over and that the Church is everywhere a
missionary body, does not our idea of preaching need a radical
conversion—a turning from incessant speaking to the faithful
few to a new effort, in the Spirit, to declare the good news in
contemporary terms to the unbelieving world?

But, in that case, what becomes of our Sunday sermons?
Such a view of preaching as that outlined above does not render
unnecessary the work among the faithful few. In the NT, after
the word had been preached and the herald had departed, the
baptised believers came under the ministry of *teachers*. It is
under the general heading of 'teaching' that our Sunday work
ought to be considered. Some parts of it are closely allied to
'preaching'. Believers need to be reminded of the gospel, to be
exhorted to a life worthy of the gospel, to be given messages
from God of judgement, hope and challenge, to be brought to
that out-working in personal responsible decision which is
conversion, to be built up. But teaching, regular and systematic, is the prime need. We give systematic teaching to the
children in the Sunday School, and, we hope, to those who are
to be received into full membership. Then the systematic
teaching stops, just when it ought to be blossoming into
maturity. Instead, we treat our congregations to a disconnected
mass of sermons. Is it not high time for those who are called
to be preachers to come together, as a group, to enquire what
the teaching ministry really *is*, to study the teaching methods of
Jesus, and strive to bring into being in our churches a fellowship of learning, in which all learn from one another, and all
are 'taught by God' (4⁹)? And what is the aim of this teaching?
As we saw in the previous *Note*, the aim is that all the saints
should be equipped for the ministry, all, as witnesses, able to
speak the word of God. For it is not only in authentic
preaching or in the ministry of teaching that human language
becomes the word of God, as it is used by Him, but in the
everyday witness of faithful Christians conversing with their
neighbours, and so fulfilling their ministry.

Before we leave this theme we must briefly touch on two
more matters. Speaking the word of God is never merely a
matter of words, even words which God uses. The word of
God '*worketh* in you that believe' (2¹³). Alongside the speaking of the word of God must go the signs of the power of His
word—changed lives, service, brotherly love, miracles of

humility and healing. The whole life of the Church ought to be, not a sign which speaks against the gospel, but a demonstration of God's power to reconcile us to Christ and so to one another.

And how, lastly, are we to know that, when we speak to the world in preaching, to the Church in teaching, or to our neighbour in witness, we are not speaking 'the word of man'? We can do no more here than refer the reader to the life of Paul, and to that OT character whom he most resembles—Jeremiah. Follow the wrestlings of Jeremiah, in such a passage as 20⁷⁻¹⁸ with the burden of the word God had given him, a word cutting directly across his natural desires and inclinations. Watch how he comes under the divine compulsion, with all the suffering it involves, a divine compulsion of which Paul's own cry is an echo, 'Woe is unto me, if I preach not the gospel' (1 Cor 9¹⁶). And study Jeremiah's encounter with the false prophets in chapter 23. They prophesy 'lies' and 'dreams' (the word of man); the true prophet stands in God's council and is sent by Him. Here are the only answers to our question— *commitment* and *prayer*.

> *Lord, if at Thy command*
> *The word of life we sow*
> *Watered by Thy almighty hand,*
> *The seed shall surely grow.* (*MHB* 792)

(2) 2¹⁷–3¹³: Loyalty on Both Sides since Parting

(a) 2¹⁷⁻²⁰: *The Thwarting of Paul's Eager Plans to Return*
Summary: *So I am accused of lack of love because I failed to return to you! I cannot exaggerate the pain of parting from you, or the eagerness of my desire to return. If it had been humanly possible, I should have been there. But Satan prevented me.*

2¹⁷. Jewish accusations of unconcern are in the background. Paul protests his love for the Thessalonians. They are more than '*brethren*'. Paul is a parent (**2⁷⁻¹¹**)—a parent '*bereaved*'. He had been forced to leave them, it is true. But the parting would be as '*short*' as he could make it; it was a parting in body only, never '*in heart*'; it was coloured by earnest endeavours and great desires to return.

D

2¹⁸. 'We did propose to come' (*NEB*). Here Paul speaks unambiguously of his own personal part in the separation.
(After all, Timothy *had* returned) '. . . *once and again*'—better,
'more than once' (*NEB*). '*Satan hindered us*'. The exact nature
of the hindrance is not clear. Something affecting Paul and not
Timothy. '*Satan*'. He is the tempter (3⁵), the Evil One, probably (2 Thess 3³). For Paul, life was a fight between the forces
of God and evil forces, with Satan at their head. The decisive
victory had been won at the Cross; the final victory would be
won at His coming. But between D-Day and V-Day Satan had
power to hinder Paul's plans to return—perhaps, even, through
his tempting, to make the whole Thessalonian campaign *in
vain* (3⁵). See *GPL, Note* 17, p. 82.

2¹⁹⁻²⁰. Now the emotion of *v.* 17 and the frustration of *v.* 18
break out into direct address to the beloved children. But, as
everywhere in these letters, what Paul says is related to '*our
Lord Jesus Christ at his coming*'. Before that Lord, the Thessalonians are said to be Paul's '*hope*', '*joy*' (twice), 'crown of
boasting' (*RSV*), and '*glory*'. Those without Christ are without '*hope*' (4¹³). But 'the God of hope' (Rom 15¹³) has given
us 'good hope through grace' (2 Thess 2¹⁶). Hope is to the
future what faith is to the present—the complete assurance that
the Lord who triumphed through the Cross, and reigns in the
present, is Lord also of the future. His victory, Paul is confident, will be revealed in the Thessalonians (5²⁴). A time will
come when Paul will present them to the coming Lord, saved
by grace (cf. 2 Cor 11², Col 1²⁸). In this assurance, they are
called Paul's '*hope*'. This presentation of converts will be '*joy*'.
They will be his '*crown of glorying*' ('boasting', *RSV*) '*before
our Lord Jesus Christ at his coming*'. In a religion of grace, of
course, boasting is excluded (Rom 3²⁷). But that in Paul which,
before his conversion, caused him to boast (Gal 1¹⁴) was not
merely removed, but was gloriously transformed into glorying
'in the cross' (Gal 6¹⁴; see *KG* 72), being proud 'in Christ
Jesus'—of what Christ had wrought through him (Rom
15¹⁷⁻¹⁸). This boasting is a selfless, satisfying thanksgiving to
Christ for what He has done for Paul and through Paul.
Christ at His coming, like some Greek king at *his* coming, is
thought of as giving signs of appreciation and praise ('Well
done, good and faithful servant', Mt 25²¹); i.e. '*a crown of
glorying*'—a crown of which a man might feel proud. But

Paul's *'crown of glorying'* is to be Christ's recognition of His own achievement through Paul—the salvation of the Thessalonians.

'coming'. The first of six occurrences of the word *parousia* in our Epistles. *'Are not even ye'*, or 'you also', probably sets the Thessalonians along with others as Paul's hoped-for *'joy'* (cf. Phil 4⁴). *'glory'*. Paul sought no glory from men **(2⁶)**. His glory (honour, praise) is to come from Christ alone. But the glory of the future is reflected back into the present. Those who will be his *'joy'* are his glory now.

Note 5: Satan

We meet Satan in three places in these epistles. (*1*) In **2¹⁸** the obstacles, whatever they were, which prevented Paul's return to Thessalonica are attributed to Satanic 'hindering'. There is sermon-material in this idea of hindering. In Acts 16⁶⁻⁷ Paul encountered hindrances, but they were the hindrances of the Holy Spirit! The Church faces many obstacles today. The preacher must give a theological interpretation of them. If this is to be true to the Bible, he must distinguish between those obstacles which are due to the attempts of Evil to thwart the will of God, and those which are due to the attempts of the Holy Spirit to thwart the self-will of the Church. (*2*) In 3¹⁻⁵ we meet Satan in his capacity of 'the tempter'. So seriously does Paul take the power of temptation in a persecution situation that he actually reckons with the possibility that all the work at Thessalonica might come to nothing. (*3*) In 2 Thess 2⁹⁻¹⁰ the power of Satan is seen to be at the back of all the activity of the man of sin. Behind the mythological language of this obscure passage lies the Pauline conviction that Evil has the power to produce a situation so terrible that no *human* skill, authority or force can prevail against it. But though for Paul Satan is a terrible reality, yet

Hell is nigh, but God is nigher (*MHB* 246)

His belief in Satan is combined with complete faith in the Lordship of Christ now, and complete hope that, when all human ingenuity fails, Christ, with glorious ease, will win His final victory (2 Thess 2⁸).

The faith underlying these three passages is the faith of the whole NT (see *GPL* 56 f). Jesus encountered a whole kingdom of evil, with Satan at its head. He took Satan with complete seriousness as a personal power aiming to prevent the coming of the Kingdom through the suffering life and death of the Messiah. From the Temptation to the Cross Jesus fought against Satan, and won the decisive victory. 'I beheld Satan fallen as lightning from heaven' (Lk 10[18]). 'Now shall the prince of this world be cast out' (Jn 12[31]). But the *decisive* victory over Satan is not the *final* victory. Satan is still alive, active in persecution, temptation, attempts to thwart the plan of God and destroy the faith of the Church. But the decisive victory *has* taken place. And because the decisive victory has taken place, however hopeless the situation may appear to be we may, in Christ, hope for the final victory. The NT never speculates on how the devil came to be the devil. Its message runs—There is a power of evil. Beware! But Satan *has been* conquered, and *will be* conquered (see *GPL* 82 f).

How are we to preach these truths today? We may agree with Thielicke that in these days, while Satan's 'strategic goal remains the same, his tactical methods have altered'. If so, we must alter ours. In *The Screwtape Letters* C. S. Lewis made a notable attempt to re-present biblical truth. In one of the letters Screwtape writes to Wormwood, a junior tempter: 'The fact that devils are predominantly *comic* figures in the modern imagination will help you. If any faint suspicion of your existence begins to rise in his mind, suggest to him a picture of something in red tights, and persuade him that, since he cannot believe in that (it is an old textbook method of confusing them) he therefore cannot believe in you.' There is some biblical imagery, also, which the modern Western mind cannot take literally. A straight effort to rehabilitate such imagery may involve us in the sort of controversy which the Bible itself so markedly avoids. What we must do is proclaim the sober truth which lies *behind* biblical imagery. Evil is real and potent. Evil is not an impersonal principle, but a Power which takes that personal initiative which we call temptation. Evil is something which only Christ can destroy. Only faith in Him can enable us, as it enabled Paul and the Thessalonians, to encounter the modern equivalents of Satan's hindering and tempting, and whatever evil initiatives may await us in the future.

We need not fear that this line of interpretation will take us away from Bible truth. The Bible combines highly figurative language with complete realism. 'Your adversary the devil, as a roaring lion, walketh about, seeking whom he may devour' (1 Pet 5[8]). But there is nothing here of the man in *The Ancient Mariner* who

> *turns no more his head*
> *Because he knows, a frightful fiend*
> *Doth close behind him tread.*

Where the Bible talks about Satan it is talking about certain situations in everyday life, inviting a judgement on the evil in those situations, and challenging believers to deal with those situations in the power of Christ. There are situations involving illness (Lk 13[16], 2 Cor 12[7]), involving the blindness and sin of individuals like Peter, Judas, Ananias and Sapphira (Mk 8[33], Lk 22[3], Acts 5[3]), sexual weakness (1 Cor 7[5]), refusal to forgive an offender (2 Cor 2[11]), false teaching (2 Cor 11[14]). The victory of God over Satan in Rom 16[20] is not a mythical struggle unconnected with 'them which are causing divisions and occasions of stumbling' of whom Paul has been speaking in 16[17]. Signs of God's victory are to be seen in a proper Christian attitude to those very divisions and occasions of stumbling. Figurative language about Satan and 'the beast' abounds in *Revelation*. In fact it is talking about the evils the churches had then to face in state and society. Our preaching about Satan today will not be biblical unless, avoiding unprofitable speculation, it sets this present age under the judgement of God, and challenges the Church to vigorous action in the name of Christ and the power of the Spirit, against evil, wherever it is to be found.

Note 6: The Parousia

The traditional symbolism of Doomsday is absurdly out of place in this modern scientific age. The temptation, therefore, to remove it from the faith is almost overwhelming. Those who fall to this temptation try to translate biblical statements about the future, without remainder, into statements about the importance of the present. There is much that is useful in this line of thought. But can the translation be made 'without remainder'? Surely not, if we are to give meaning, as we must, to the idea of God as the God of time, who has a purpose in history. If history had a beginning in Creation, and a midpoint in Christ, then it must have an End. God, who won the decisive victory against evil in Christ, must also win the final victory through that same Christ. History will end worthily of God who made it. Without such a faith in such a real historical process our hope is vain.

The Church of the NT is the Church which earnestly prayed 'Maranatha' (Our Lord, *come*); the Church which waited for the Coming of the One who had already come. Only the most heroic 'exegetical chemistry' attempts to remove the idea of the victorious ending of history from the various strands of the teaching of Jesus. The hope of the Parousia sounds throughout the NT. In some places the stress is more on the truth 'that the One who has come will come' (e.g. *Matthew, Revelation* and our epistles). In other places the stress is more on the truth 'that the One who will come is the One who has come'. This is especially true of the Fourth Gospel, which reminds a Church troubled about the delay of the 'future Coming', that He has already come. He came in the resurrection, in the coming of the Paraclete. Father and Son 'come' wherever there is real love issuing in obedience (Jn 14^{23}). But even in the Fourth Gospel the future coming is not removed (Jn 14^3, 5$^{28-9}$; see *OEE* 57 f).

The real problem is that in much of the NT the Coming is thought to be *near*, and is expected *soon*. 4^{17} and 1 Cor 15^{51} clearly mean that Paul, when he wrote those words, expected the Coming to take place in his own lifetime. Among the recorded sayings of Jesus there are three (Mk 9^1, Mt 10^{23}, Mk 13^{30}) which could easily give rise to this expectation (see *CLM* and *AMW*). It is not for this commentary to discuss what Jesus meant by these sayings, and how far the Church's expectation of a near coming is a misunderstanding of what He said. The expectation was *there*. Jn 21$^{20-3}$ speaks to a church holding on tenaciously to the belief that He would come while at least *one* of His disciples was still alive. But the belief was mistaken. He simply did not come in that generation (see *OEE* 223; *GPL* 61 f, 72 f).

Now it might be expected that, once this fact had become clear, the Church would cease talking about the nearness of the End. But this in fact is not the case. The Church continued to transmit the Lord's sayings which had given rise to the belief about the nearness of the End, long after it had become clear that they were not to be interpreted as a literal prophecy of a Coming 'in this generation'. The Church was disappointed, but not devastated. The word 'near' had to be interpreted in some other sense than 'chronologically soon'. We must hear and take to heart the saying of Jesus about 'this generation'. It speaks to each and every generation. The teaching about the Coming is not concerned with some unknown and distant era. It concerns you and me here and now. But what in fact does 'the Coming is near' mean if not 'the Coming is to happen soon'? The word 'near' is to be interpreted with reference to the difference made to the world by the first Coming of Christ. The Cross and Resurrection are seen in the Bible as 'eschatological' events which brought the world into a new age. In them God won the decisive victory over evil. The world can never be the same again. The rest is epilogue. So, however long, in the mercy of God (2 Pet 3⁹) the End is chronologically delayed, it is still near because the decisive events have already happened and the victory only remains to be consummated.

Of course the event which brings history as we know it to an end is not an historical event like any other. It has no successor. History is at an end. But this is not the main point. The Coming of the Son of Man is the symbol of the transformation of history into the eternal kingdom of God. And because this is an event utterly outside human experience, it can only be spoken about at all in symbols. The 'traditional symbolism' of Doomsday is, therefore, an attempt to describe what cannot in any case be described, and perhaps our efforts at 're-mythologizing' will not be any better than the Bible's 'myths'! Our epistles are, in fact, instructive here. Even for Paul the symbolism in itself is not the most important thing. On the occasions in which he speaks about the Parousia he selects, from the available store of apocalyptic symbolism, just what he needs for his purpose at the moment. For the bereaved he describes the Coming in relation to the gathering of dead and living (4¹³⁻¹⁸); for those who asked 'When?' he describes it in its aspect of suddenness (5¹⁻¹¹); for the persecuted he describes it as judgement (2 Thess 1¹⁻¹⁰); and for those who thought they knew the time he describes it as preceded by signs (2 Thess 2¹⁻¹²). His concern with the symbolism is the concern, first and foremost, of a pastor. It should be ours, too.

'The meaning of the NT thought about the Parousia is that
the tension between what has been fulfilled and what remains
unfulfilled; between this world and that; between hoping and
having; the hidden and the revealed; faith and sight—will be
resolved, and that for such a resolving of tension the decisive
thing has already taken place in Christ.' (Oepke in Kittel's
Wörterbuch.) On the basis of this faith we must preach the two
great Christian themes—the *hope* that He who has won the
victory will win the victory, and the *urgency* that calls us, in the
knowledge that the time is both limited and unknown, to
abound in the work of the Lord.

> *Yea, Amen! Let all adore Thee, High on Thy eternal*
> *throne;*
> *Saviour take the power and glory, Claim the kingdom*
> *for Thine own;*
> *Hallelujah! Everlasting God, come down! (MHB 264)*

(b) 3¹⁻⁵: *The Sending of Timothy*

Summary: *Satan was at work in Athens, hindering my journey
to you. I was afraid that Satan's work in Thessalonica
might wreck the whole mission. The situation was intolerable. I was forced to make the costly and difficult decision
to send Timothy.*

3¹. '*Wherefore when we could no longer forbear*'—Paul was
forced to choose between evils, either to leave the Thessalonians
without the needed contact, or to deprive himself of the services
of Timothy—'*we thought it good to be left behind at Athens
alone*'; in *v*. 5 Paul says, '*I also, when I could no longer forbear,
sent . . .*' These verses raise acutely the meaning of '*we*' in these
letters. They are written in the name of Paul, Silvanus and
Timothy. When Paul writes '*we*' does he always consciously
include the other two, or does he, at least sometimes, use '*we*'
in the sense of '*I*'? The interesting (and insoluble) problem is
whether the use of the plural in this verse allows us to infer that
Silvanus had come to Athens and was involved in the decision
to send Timothy. Probably not. We have already concluded
that the letter is Paul's, and not 'committee-drafting' (see comment on 1¹). Paul may well use 'we' when he means 'I'. And if
Silvanus was still with Paul in Athens, does he not 'protest too
much' about the difficulty of sending Timothy? It seems likely

that, in answer to Paul's request of Acts 17[15], Timothy came, but Silvanus (hindered by God or by Satan!) did not.

3[2]. Paul's decision to send Timothy was hard for him; it should be valued by the Thessalonians. For Timothy is 'our brother'; not only a fellow Christian, but a valued colleague. There is uncertainty in the MSS. about the next words. We think Paul wrote the magnificent words 'God's fellow-worker in the service of the gospel of Christ' (*NEB*), and that later copyists toned this down to '*God's minister*'. Perhaps Paul wrote to show the true worth of a man who had not played a prominent part in the Thessalonian mission, and is not even mentioned in Acts 17[1–10]. So much for Timothy the man. His mission is to '*establish*'. The man who established is a true worker with God, for it is God who 'establishes' (3[13], 2 Thess 2[17], 3[3]). '*comfort*' properly means 'strengthen', and strengthening is the work of the Holy Spirit. '*concerning your faith*'. The exact sense is not clear. The *NEB* translation 'stand firm for the faith' is surely wrong. The general meaning is that Timothy is so to administer God's strengthening that the faith of the Thessalonians may grow.

3[3–4]. Timothy's mission was necessary because the Thessalonians were in a persecution situation, and would hear that Paul was similarly placed. Such a situation gives an opportunity for God's strengthening—but also the danger that the persecuted will be '*moved*'. This word occurs only here in the NT. It is used of a dog wagging its tail and *fawning*, and so can have the meaning of being 'beguiled' (*NEB* margin) and so 'cajoled into disloyalty'. The idea would be that 'the tempter', through his agents, the Jews, might take subtle advantage of the situation to seduce the Thessalonians from the faith. But perhaps the meaning 'be shaken' is preferable—the opposite of standing 'fast in the Lord' (3[8]). Timothy's mission is to remind them of what they already knew about affliction. There is a 'divine must' about it for the Christian—we are 'appointed' or destined to it (cf. Lk 2[34], Phil 1[16], Mk 8[31]). This had been the teaching given by Paul in Thessalonica; the Thessalonians have good reason to know how true his teaching was.

3[5]. Paul now goes back to amplify *v.* 1. In an intolerable situation he chose to send Timothy. What he wanted was news of how the faith of the Thessalonians was standing the test. What he feared was nothing less than the possibility that Satan's temptings might be too subtle and too strong, and that all the labour of the Thessalonian mission might come to nothing.

N.B. For 3^{1-5}, see also *Note 5*.

Note 7: Suffering

Paul and his companions came to Thessalonica having suffered in Philippi (2^2), prepared for further suffering. In his preaching, Paul did not hide from the Thessalonians the truth that following Christ meant suffering affliction (3^4). He wrote the letters from Corinth in continuing '*distress and affliction*' (3^7). The Thessalonians, having counted the cost, 'received the word', and found that Paul's warning was true (3^4). Christianity meant suffering for them also (1^6, 2^{14}, 3^3, 2 Thess $1^{4, 6, 7}$). The epistles give the following message about suffering—

(*a*) It is unavoidable for the Christian—'*hereunto we are appointed*' (3^3). We are to be suffering servants of the Suffering Servant.

(*b*) Christians who suffer are imitators of Paul (1^6), of 'the churches of God' from the beginning (2^{14}), 'of the Lord' (1^6). (This hint of suffering as imitators of the Lord is developed in later letters into teaching about 'the fellowship of his sufferings', which comes to its finest expression in Col 1^{24} and 2 Cor 1^{3-7} (see *HKM* 23 f).

(*c*) A realistic point—suffering is a temptation to Christians, an opportunity for Satan to attempt his work of destruction (3^5). But—

(*d*) sufferings are also an opportunity for the Christian ministry of 'establishing' and 'comforting'—Christ's way of building up His Church (3^2).

(*e*) Where sufferings are accepted in Christian faith, they become the raw material of notable Christian graces—'joy of the Holy Ghost' (1^6); and especially *hypomene* (translated *patience*), not a passive resignation, but a victorious God-given spirit of overcoming. This '*patience*' the Thessalonians have—'patience of hope' (1^3). For this Paul gives thanks to God (2 Thess 1^4), and prays for further supplies of it (2 Thess 3^5). Finally—

(*f*) Sufferings are eschatological—pointing towards the

coming victory. 'Let us also rejoice in our tribulations', says Paul, 'knowing that tribulation worketh patience; and patience, probation; and probation, hope' (Rom 5³⁻⁴). 'The patience of hope' in the midst of persecution and tribulation is 'a manifest token of the righteous judgement of God' (2 Thess 1⁵).

What does all this mean for us today—especially in places where Christians are no longer persecuted, but tolerated, pitied and ignored? To us suffering means pain—cancer, motor smashes, sudden death. These are not Paul's theme. These are part of life, for Christians and non-Christians alike, to be fought against in Christian service, or borne with faith and courage if they come. But it is part of the task of the preacher to *prepare* people for this kind of suffering. Many people go down under it because they are not prepared. Should we not teach people to *expect* suffering, and help them to see and to understand the various reactions to it? There are the negative destructive reactions of bitterness and resentment to which Satan tempts (3⁵). There is the passive resignation which remains unfruitful. There is the creative attitude which accepts suffering with courage and faith—'God is with me, and can and will turn it into good for me' (1⁶, 2 Thess 1⁴, Rom 5³⁻⁴). But there is also a faith which goes deeper and believes that suffering offered up to God is somehow used in His mysterious purposes for the world (Col 1²⁴, 2 Cor 1³⁻⁷). Above all else, the sufferer needs to believe that there can be *meaning* in his suffering. Can we help him to find this in 'the fellowship of his sufferings'?

But when Paul here speaks of sufferings he means the inevitable consequences of the sort of faith we find in Epistles such as these. When Love comes unarmed into a world of clashing self-centredness, Love must suffer—and through suffering, conquer. We also are in the same world. We are summoned to a new experience of conversion—to God, to one another, to the world—with the warning that such a faith, such love, even in this present age, *especially* in this present age, will bring suffering, and that only if we accept the suffering can we expect the victory to take place—in us, and in that part of His work for which we are responsible. There are suffering churches in the world today. Let us, as we conduct worship, help our congregations to share their suffering, at least to the extent of costly intercession. But more than that, should we not seek to discover what it means in the world of today—amid race conflict and hunger, for instance—to be 'suffering servants of the Suffering Servant'? And should we not ask whether, if we are not suffering, we are avoiding that to which 'we are appointed' (3³)?

> *Thee, Jesus, full of truth and grace,*
> *Thee, Saviour, we adore,*
> *Thee in affliction's furnace praise,*
> *And magnify Thy power.*
>
> *Thy power, in human weakness shown,*
> *Shall make us all entire;*
> *We now Thy guardian presence own,*
> *And walk unburned in fire. (MHB 519)*

(c) 3⁶⁻¹⁰: *Good News*

Summary: *And now Timothy has come with the good news that your faith and love have stood the test! Our enforced separation has not harmed our personal relationships. I hardly know how to express my joy and thankfulness to God. My prayers for a return to you have increased still further in intensity.*

3⁶. Paul writes, immediately after the arrival of Timothy, in the first flush of his joy. The writing of *1 Thessalonians* is thus anchored at Acts 18⁵. He calls the news brought by Timothy '*glad tidings*', making use of a verb which is elsewhere used exclusively of the preaching of the Christian good news, the gospel. But the verb is used not improperly—for Timothy's news was of the 'gospel in action'. It was in two parts.

(*a*) In spite of Paul's departure and in spite of persecution, there were in Thessalonica the two fundamental signs of the Christian life, '*faith*' and '*love*'—the faith which is a personal relationship with the living Christ, the love through which faith works (Gal 5⁶). (The third member of Paul's famous trio is missing here, perhaps because, as we shall see, the 'hope' of the Thessalonians was not in so healthy a state as their faith and love.)

(*b*) The second part of the glad tidings was personal—the Thessalonians were as eager to see Paul as he was to see them.

3⁷. Now the triad is reduced to the 'one thing needful'—'*faith*'. Paul is '*comforted*' (i.e. strengthened, reassured, *NEB*) in all his '*distress*' and '*affliction*'. There are signs that Paul had felt the strain of life since leaving Thessalonica. To the pain of that parting was added another from Beroea; and yet another from Timothy in Athens, when he could 'bear it no longer'. Alone he faced the religiosity of the Athenian intellectuals on the Areopagus. In spite of some success (Acts 17[34]), he went hurriedly on to Corinth, a city notorious for its immorality. He reached there in weakness, fear and much trembling—determined not to know anything among them, save Jesus Christ and Him crucified (1 Cor 2[2–3]). It seems likely that we ought to infer that, in addition to all the other elements of strain, Paul was troubled about the methods he had employed at Athens. Had he been too intellectual? Had he failed to proclaim the Crucified with sufficient directness? It has been suggested that he might have determined to regard Thessalonica as a sort of test of his methods. If all this is so, we can readily understand the extent of his relief at Timothy's '*glad tidings*'.

3[8]. The strain under which he had lived had been a sort of death. Now he has a new lease of life at the news of the Thessalonians' faith—here alternatively described as standing '*fast in the Lord*'. They are 'in the Lord', in personal relationship with Him (and with all others 'in Him'); and that relationship has remained rock-like in the storms of persecution (Mt 7[25]).

3[9]. Paul's joy at this is not only natural, human joy; it is joy before God (in whose presence there is fulness of joy, Ps 16[11]). Such joy demands a 'rendering again' of thanks, i.e. giving God the thanks which are His due. But so great is the gift that Paul despairs of due thanksgiving.

3[10]. With the thanksgiving part of his prayer goes a continual ('*night and day*') and intense (the word translated '*exceedingly*' expressed the very limit of human intensity) petition that God may allow him to see them again and '*perfect that which is lacking*' in their faith. The Thessalonian church is a model church, Paul's glory and joy. But Paul's love is realistic; he is well aware that there are gaps in the church's faith, and that his work is not yet done. Faith in its fundamentals is simple—the receiving by the penitent sinner of God's gift of relationship with Himself. But

> *When the work is done,*
> *The work is but begun:* (*MHB* 105)

The believer needs to experience the fulness of God's gift and
God's demand. For this he needs to understand what God has
done (theology) and how He wills His children to live (ethics).
Our present-day 'missionary methods' are often contrasted
very unfavourably with Paul's. Paul stayed in a place for a
short time only; then departed, commending the church he had
established to the Lord (Acts 14²³), entrusting its future to the
Holy Spirit. We, however, tend to regard as normal that con-
tradiction in terms—a 'mission-station'. There is much truth
in this contrast. But, on the other hand, we should note that
Paul does not consider his work in Thessalonica to be complete
at his departure.

Note 8: Prayer

This section shows us Paul *'praying exceedingly'*. Let us
collect together what our Epistles have to tell us about the life
of prayer.

There is, first of all, *intercession*. Paul prays for the Thessalonians (1², 2 Thess 1¹¹) 'constantly', 'always'; and humbly asks
for their prayers for him (5²⁵, 2 Thess 3¹). Christian life is
family life. By this ministry of intercession love among the
members lives and grows (see *KG* 83).

Then there is *petition*. This passage is instructive. Paul prays
with a 'Gethsemane intensity' (3¹⁰) that the mysterious hindering of Satan (2¹⁸) may be removed, so that he may come to
Thessalonica. But, having prayed, he leaves the issue, in
Gethsemane faith, to God. In fact, as we have seen, God said
'not yet'. This is the Lord's prayer, pattern of Paul's prayers.
And this pattern he teaches to others, as we see in 2 Thess 3¹, ²:
'brethren, pray for us, that the word of the Lord may run and
be glorified . . . and that we may be delivered'. *First*, God's
kingdom; *then*, our needs.

Finally there is *thanksgiving*. The Paul of these letters
abounds in thanksgiving. He gives thanks *'always'* (1²), *'without ceasing'* (2¹³), *'alway'* (2 Thess 1³, 2¹³), while in 3⁹ he
despairs of finding words adequate to express his thankfulness.
All this practice comes to sharp focus in his precept in 5¹⁸—
'In everything give thanks' ('in all circumstances', *RSV*, 'what-

ever happens', *NEB*). We are not only to thank God when something nice happens to us! Paul's greatest outbursts of thanksgiving come in the most adverse circumstances—e.g. 2 Cor 1³⁻⁴, 'in all our affliction'; Eph 1³⁻¹⁴ (written from prison). The reason, of course, is that there is nothing self-centred in Paul's thanksgivings. In all the Thessalonian references he is thanking God for what He has done in other people. Everything points to the main theme—'Thanks be to God for his unspeakable gift' (2 Cor 9¹⁵). As this is their content, Paul's thanksgivings are independent of personal circumstances. He can give thanks 'in all circumstances, whatever happens'. It is not that we are to give thanks *for* all things. That cannot be, as long as there are sin and evil in the world. But *in* whatever circumstances we may be, we know that God is with us, and that He is stronger than evil. The true Christian, then, will give thanks, even *in* tribulation—*for* God's presence, His power to cope with the situation, and the challenge of it (2 Cor 4¹⁷).

The final, and the deepest, teaching of *Thessalonians* about prayer comes in 5¹⁷—'*pray without ceasing*'. Few texts call more urgently these days for explanation than this. We have already, in this note, looked at Paul's account of his own prayer life. He intercedes, asks, gives thanks, '*always*', '*constantly*', '*without ceasing*'. May we not interpret this to mean that Paul had settled habits of prayer, praying not 'when he felt like it' but at certain times, regularly set apart? And may we not begin our interpretation of '*pray without ceasing*' here? Is not the first step the cultivation of these settled prayer-habits? The answer is, of course, that we cannot, these days, take so much for granted. In view of current teaching about prayer, we must go further back and ask 'What is prayer?' and 'Why is it necessary?'

In *Note* 1, we looked briefly at the admirable revolt of the 'New Theology' against the idea of God as 'up there' 'out there', at the circumference of life, rather than at its centre. But we suggested that the end product of this revolt, the idea of God as 'the Ground of our being' or 'the Beyond in the midst' did less than justice to the biblical message. The inadequacy of this idea is seen most clearly in the teaching of the New Theology about prayer. We take the fifth chapter of *Honest to God* as an example of this teaching. If 'God out there' is replaced by 'the Ground of our being', what becomes of prayer? In another context Bishop Robinson can say, 'I would wish to affirm the centrality of the utterly personal communion with God summed up in the "Abba, Father".' But in *Honest to God* it is precisely this personal communion which is lacking. Terms like 'Ground' or 'the Beyond' are much less personal that the biblical terms. Relationship with a Ground or a Beyond is much more like relationship with an 'It' rather than a 'Him'. God is not to be cultivated by withdrawal from life into some hidden garden. He is to be met *here*, in matters of most concern, in work, service, personal relationships. The result is that, although it is admitted that times of disengagement from the life of work and service are necessary, it is the times of engagement that really matter. Times of disengagement are, in the words of Bishop Robinson, 'times of standing back, of consolidation, of letting love's roots grow'. (Bishop Newbigin describes them as 'a sort of gathering together of faculties for the next encounter with the world'.) The 'moment of revelation' (to return to Bishop Robinson), 'the pentecostal point is the engagement'. And so it is natural enough to find Bishop Robinson advocating the following form of training. 'I would start the other end in teaching the discipline of prayer—not from '*chronos*', time set by the clock, but from '*kairos*', i.e. waiting for the moment which drives us to our knees.'

What are we to say to all this? Surely three things.

1. If we are to translate what the Bible actually says, we must interpret prayer not as activity but as communion with God. Until we get God right, we can never get prayer right. God is the Other, over against us. Prayer is dialogue, talking with the Father. And personal relationships cannot grow unless they are deliberately cultivated.

2. While it is true and important to say that it is not necessary to withdraw from the world to find God, it *is* necessary to withdraw from ourselves and our works to submit them to His judgement and grace. It is only in the encounter of faith, when our works become the works of the Spirit, that they are of any value.

3. The '*kairoi*', the unplanned moments of life, the moments which drive us to our knees are, of course, of the utmost importance. But it is only on a basis of '*chronoi*'—times habitually, deliberately, painfully set aside for communion with the Father—that we can recognize and make use of the *kairoi* when they come.

But, even if it is true that 'pray without ceasing' must begin here, where it began for Paul, it must not end here. 'Pray without ceasing' is something that gives unity to the whole of life, binding together the times of communion with God and the life of service to God in service of neighbour; a life, to quote Bishop Newbigin, 'in which all our acts are simply acted prayers to God for the doing of His will, and all our prayers look for their answers in the affairs of the secular world'. D. T. Niles put the matter thus: 'It is wise to maintain both the prayer-dimension of work as well as the work-dimension of prayer. Prayer is also something one must do. Why cannot it be that there are stated times each day for prayer—times that are *chronoi*—when one prays as a habit and as a routine, be the time spent long or short or very short? And why cannot it be that each day there are also extended periods of prayer— periods that are *kairoi*—when work and witness spill over into prayer and there is unhurried waiting upon God? And why cannot work and prayer be joined by acts of ejaculatory prayer that make work an expression of thankfulness to God and make prayer the offering of our work?'

The life of 'pray without ceasing', where prayer and work are woven into one harmonious whole, is not achieved without struggle and toil. The difficulty of prayer in this present age is often seen as a reason for giving up the effort. But it must rather be seen as a challenge. Yet the life of prayer is not a matter of effort but of grace. Our Epistle in 'pray without ceasing', 'in everything give thanks', sets the problem but does not specifically provide the solution. For that we must look to other Epistles—to Rom 8[26-7], Eph 6[18], to 'prayer in the Spirit', prayer not so much as something we do, as something the Holy Spirit does within us (see *VT* 54 f; *HKM* 132 f).

> *Come in Thy pleading Spirit down*
>   *To us who for Thy coming stay;*
> *Of all Thy gifts we ask but one,*
>   *We ask the constant power to pray:*
> *Indulge us, Lord, in this request;*
> *Thou canst not then deny the rest.* (*MHB* 534)

(d) 3[11-13]: *A Prayer*
Summary: *May God and Christ (in their unity) remove the*

E

obstacles in the way which leads me to you. May the Lord fill you to overflowing with true Christian love.

3¹¹. Satan put obstacles in Paul's way **(2¹⁸).** Paul prays to the One who is able to remove those obstacles. The prayer is to '*our God and Father himself*' (revealed as 'our Father' in Jesus Christ His only Son) and '*our Lord Jesus*', His only Son, made man as Jesus, made 'Lord' by God (Acts 2³⁶), the object of Christian allegiance and worship. But now comes a very interesting thing. The prayer is made to 'our God' and 'our Lord'. We should expect Paul to write 'may *they* direct our way'. But he does not. He writes, 'may *He* direct'. The subject is plural, the verb singular. In the artless outpouring of his devotion, Paul gives expression to the truth otherwise expressed as 'I and the Father are one' (John 10³⁰), and as the doctrine of the Holy Trinity. Another interesting point, on which we must reflect, is that Paul does not seem to have visited Thessalonica again for many years—till Acts 20¹⁻². God's answer to prayer is not always 'yes'. He may say 'no' (Mk 14³⁶, 2 Cor 12⁸); or, as here, 'not yet'.

3¹². Paul has made his earnest petition to be allowed to return to Thessalonica. He now leaves the answer entirely to God, and goes on to pray serenely for the Thessalonians. Whether He uses Paul's return, or some other way, it is God who must perfect what is lacking in their faith. Paul prays that the Lord may do this by giving them '*love*'. They already *have* love **(1³),** but it is not enough to *have* it; it must '*increase and abound*'. The love for which he prays is not the natural human affection which loves a few, and loves those few for a reason; it is the love which loves *all* the members of the congregation, and 'all men', including, of course, their persecutors. Such love is the *agape* of God, 'poured into our hearts through the Holy Spirit' (Rom 5⁵). This miracle has happened to Paul, and again he can humbly put himself forward as a witness.

3¹³. This flooding of the heart with love is the way by which God leads the believer to the ultimate goal—the establishment of the heart in 'holiness'. Heart is not confined, in the Bible, to the emotional part of the personality; it embraces the whole personality, mind, affection and will. Establishing is something Timothy was sent to do **(3²),** and no doubt God used him for that purpose; but the ultimate strengthening of the personality in the Christian life is the work of God (cf. 1 Pet 5¹⁰). The root idea of *'holiness'* is being set apart for God, made available for the doing of His work, the living of His life. When a man by faith accepts God's grace in Christ, he *is* set apart for God. The rest of his life is the realization of what is implicit in his conversion—the more and more complete showing forth in his deeds and life of that consecration which is already his in Christ. Holiness is the life of those who have been saved from self and given to God; which is why the love which directs the life from self to God and the neighbour is such an essential part of it. Paul's prayer is directed towards the ultimate encounter of the believer with God at the Judgement. He dares to pray that in that encounter they may be found *'unblameable'*. Paul uses this word of his pre-conversion days when he was blameless according to the righteousness of the law (Phil 3⁶; see *KG* 104). He has also said that, by grace, his life at Thessalonica was blameless before God who proves the heart (2¹⁰, 2⁴). He prays that this may be true of all the Thessalonian believers— that at the Last Judgement God may have no fault to find with them, and may say, 'Well done' (Mt 25²³); that they may be like the soul which

> *When placed within Thy searching sight*
> *It shrinks not, but, with calm delight*
> *Can live, and look on Thee.* (*MHB* 544)

The immediate prelude to the Judgement is *'the Coming'* (never far from Paul's thoughts in these letters). The Lord Jesus will come *'with all his saints'*. *'saints'* in the NT usually means believers, some of whom will accompany the Lord at His coming (4¹⁴). But there is an echo in this verse of Zech 14⁵, where 'holy ones' means angels. For the coming of the Lord with angels, see 2 Thess 1⁷ and Mk 8³⁸. Here 'saints' seems to include both believers and angels. *NEB* well translates 'with all those who are his own'.

N.B. For more about this prayer, see *Note* 19.

(B) 4^1–5^{24}: The Life of Holiness, Love and Hope

WE now come to the second part of the letter. Many of Paul's letters are divided into two parts, usually called 'the theological part' and 'the ethical part'. We think, for instance, of *Romans* (break at 12^1), *Colossians* (break at 3^1), *Ephesians* (break at 4^1). See *VT, HKM*. These two parts are, of course, very closely joined together. Paul knows of no theology which does not issue in ethics, no ethics not rooted in theology. But usually he speaks first of the truths of the gospel, then of the life which follows from faith in the gospel. This is roughly the pattern of this Epistle. In **1–3** he has been thanking God for what had happened in Thessalonica; in **4** and **5** he takes up the problems reported by Timothy from the Thessalonian church. But for the most part these problems are concerned with Christian living, so that chapters **4** and **5** sketch the life involved in such thanksgiving as is described in chapters **1** to **3**. Or we may describe the chapters as the way by which God leads His Church to the holiness prayed for in 3^{13}.

(1) 4^{1-12}: The Life Pleasing to God

(a) 4^{1-2}: *Abounding Obedience*
Summary: *You know the sort of life you ought to live; you are living it; press on to more perfect obedience still!*

4^1. The word translated '*finally*' need mean no more than a transition to another point. 'Furthermore' (*AV*), or 'And now' (*NEB*) would be better.

'*brethren*'. Paul's affection can be seen in the whole verse—and also the fact that he is dictating the letter! For he starts off '*we beseech and exhort you in the Lord Jesus, that, as ye received of us how ye ought to walk and to please God*'—and presumably intended to say 'you should so walk'. But, in mid-sentence, with tact and affection, he says 'as you are in fact walking', and confines his asking and beseeching to '*abound more and more*'. There are several points here.

(*a*) Paul not only 'handed on' the gospel (1 Cor 15[1]) but also gave ethical instructions about how believers must live.

(*b*) Christian living is again (cf. **2**[12]) a '*walk*'—but, unlike that of the Jews (**2**[15]) a 'walk pleasing to God'.

(*c*) But the instructions about the Christian life are not a new sort of law—the sort of law which you can 'obey and be done with'—but something in which it is possible to '*abound more and more*'.

(*d*) Instructions have been given. Paul's task is to '*beseech and exhort*'. And this he does '*in the Lord Jesus*'; not 'off his own bat', but in virtue of the new relationships to the Lord and to the believers into which faith has brought him.

4[2]. He reminds them of the '*charge*' ('orders', *NEB*) he gave them. The word is used of a military order sent by one in authority to the troops, expecting obedience. But the 'orders' were given, not on the authority of Paul, but '*through the Lord Jesus*'. This is not different from 'in the Lord Jesus' in *v*. 1. Through Paul the Lord gives His 'standing orders' to His army.

(b) 4[3-8]: *Sexual Purity*

Summary: *The Christian's whole life, including his sexual life, must be given to God. God not only demands this; He invites us into a new life where it becomes a real possibility.*

The Thessalonians were walking according to the orders of Christ mediated through Paul (*v*. 1). So the background of this section is not to be found in actual sexual irregularities in the congregation. But Timothy had no doubt reported, what in any case Paul must have known, that they were grievously tempted. The lax sexual morality of the day can be seen from passages like the following, from very reputable authors, chosen almost at random. Plutarch in his 'advice on marriage' says that a wife should not be angry with her husband for 'some intrigue with a harlot or maidservant; she should reflect that he is indulging his wantonness and gratifying his passion with another woman out of respect for herself'. Demosthenes writes as follows: 'We keep prostitutes for pleasure; we keep mistresses for the day to day needs of the body; we keep wives for the begetting of children and for the faithful guardianship of our homes'. In addition, in much Greek religion, perhaps in certain cults in Thessalonica itself, fornication and lust were given a place in 'sacred' ritual. To new Christians, struggling to walk so as to please God in such an atmosphere, Paul writes.

4³. We have had the 'orders' of Christ and the exhortations of Paul. Behind these is the will of the holy God who acts to fulfil His will. His will is our *'sanctification'*.

> *He wills that I should holy be;*
> *What can withstand His will?*
> *The counsel of His grace in me*
> *He surely shall fulfil.* (*MHB* 565)

In 3¹³ Paul had prayed that, at the Last Judgement, the Thessalonians may be declared to be 'unblameable in holiness'. This is the end of a process of which the beginning is *faith*, the faith by which the believer is, in Christ, consecrated or set aside for God to use. In between this beginning and this end lies a time during which, by God's grace, the believers consecrated to Him become progressively more suitable for His use. An indispensable part of this sanctification is to *'abstain from fornication'*, i.e. to make a clean break with any sort of sexual activity other than what God has sanctified in holy matrimony.

4⁴⁻⁶ᵃ. Now we come to one of the main difficulties of interpretation in this Epistle. Paul is explaining what he means by 'abstaining from fornication' in *v.* 3. He uses the phrase *'possess himself of his own vessel'* (or, more literally, 'get his own vessel'). From very early times interpreters have been divided about the meaning of these words. Some support the *RSV* translation 'take a wife'; others the *NEB* translation 'gain mastery over his body'. Arguments are complicated and evenly balanced. It seems best to set out the different interpretations (none of which is without interest to the preacher).

The most recent exponent of the *RSV* interpretation is Maurer (in Kittel's *Theological Wordbook*. He believes that two Hebrew expressions lie behind the phrase translated 'get his own vessel'—one a phrase meaning 'take a wife' (e.g. Deut 21¹³, 24¹); the other a Jewish way of speaking of sexual life through the metaphor of a vessel. Paul is intending to give to

the Thessalonians, in their difficult situation, the teaching of
1 Cor 7² —'because of fornication, let each man have his own
wife'. The passage therefore runs (*1*) Christians must abstain
from all extra-marital sex relationships (*v.* 3), (*2*) each must
know how to take a wife for himself, (*3*) understanding the
differences between Christian and Gentile marriage. The
believer must take a wife; but his marriage must be part of his
sanctification. He must *honour* his wife (cf. 1 Pet 3⁷); his
marriage must not be the use of another's body for the satisfaction of his own lusts, as is the case among the Gentiles (of
whose *culpable* ignorance of God Paul speaks in Rom 1¹⁸⁻³²).
(*4*) One thing more (in *v.* 6a)—consequently, with a truly
Christian marriage, there will be no selfish invasion of a
brother's right (e.g. by adultery) '*in the matter*' (i.e. of marriage).

The monumental French Roman Catholic commentary of
Rigaux favours the *NEB* interpretation. In this case Paul is
here giving the teaching later elaborated in 1 Cor 6¹²⁻²⁰. '*vessel*'
means 'body' (and 'body' in Paul is not only the physical frame;
it verges on what is meant by personality). The Christian must
honour his body, as 'a member of Christ' and 'a temple of the
Holy Ghost', get the mastery over it, and dedicate it to God for
His use ('*sanctification*'). The body must neither be used as a
means of gratifying lust, as pagans do, nor as a means of
selfishly wronging a brother '*in the matter*' (i.e. of sex).

Both interpretations stress that part of holiness is the com-
mittal of sexual life to the holy God.

We ought to make brief mention of one more interpretation
which translates the phrase '*in the matter*' (*v.* 6a) as 'in business'.
In this case, in *vv.* 5 and 6, Paul excludes from the life of the
Christian not only impurity but also the greed which tempts a
man to wrong his brother in money matters. It is very doubtful whether the Greek word can sustain the meaning 'business',
but Paul does often set sexual impurity and greed in money
matters side by side as the typical sins of the Gentile world
(e.g. Col 3⁵, Eph 5³; see *HKM*).

4⁶ᵇ⁻⁸. Now follow three reasons for that part of holiness
which consists in 'abstaining' (*v.* 3). (*a*) God as '*avenger*' (*v.* 6)
'*in all these things*' (i.e. in all forms of sexual aberration, or
impurity and greed, if we can accept the reference to business).
God's vengeance, like His wrath (**1¹⁰**), is that part of His love
which opposes evil. In the present, this opposition consists in

giving up the sinner to the consequences of his sin (Rom 1$^{24-6,}$ ^{28}). It will be consummated in the Judgement.

(b) God's *call* (2^{12}, 2 Thess 2^{14}). No part of the life of the believer can be considered apart from the mighty event of God's invasion of his life. The aim of God's 'apprehending' of a man is not to leave him in the impurity in which he was previously. The very fact of God's call involves '*sanctification*', and excludes its opposite.

(c) God's 'impossible' call to holiness is made possible by God's gift of the Holy Spirit (He 'giveth' *v.* 8)—given continually with each new moral challenge. Relapsing into uncleanness means 'rejecting' God, rejecting the Holy Spirit. Unthinkable!

(c) 4$^{9-12}$: *Brotherly Love and Faithfulness to Duty*
Summary: *You know that holiness involves fellowship. Press on. It also involves honest work.*

4$^{9-10}$. Holiness involves not only the 'vertical' relationship to God, but the 'horizontal' relationship to Christian brethren. Not only the negative relationship of abstention from everything that would harm them (*v.* 3), but also the positive relationship of 'love in action'. This love (*a*) is not something which can be 'taught', even by Paul, but something needing the direct action of God—(and that His direct action is taking place is shown by the love of the Thessalonians for every Christian family in Macedonia). And (*b*) this love is something which never reaches its goal, but can always increase and '*abound more and more*'.

4^{11}. These injunctions are related to the local situation, and are illustrated by the worsening of that situation described in 2 Thess 3$^{6-15}$. Timothy had no doubt reported a certain tendency to excitement, to 'busy-bodiness', and to laziness (probably caused by eschatological tension). Paul rebukes excitement with a paradox rendered by Phillips, 'make it your ambition to have no ambition' ('to be quiet'). He tells the busybodies to mind their own business (not try to interfere with God's action in each individual soul); and reminds the lazy of his charge to work with their own hands (although such work might be considered shameful by the Greeks).

4¹². There are two reasons for this way of life. The Church must not forget its obligation to those outside. The 'outsider' is to be called in by the quality of life of the Christian community. '. . . *have need of nothing*'—better, *RSV* 'be dependent on nobody'. 'Christ commands us to be charitable . . . but He tells us plainly that to *count* upon charity, except in the case of necessity, is both sinful and shameful. (*Denney*)

Note 9: Holiness

God is holy: negatively in the sense of being eternally separated from evil and sin; and positively, in being endowed with that indescribable quality, the proper response to which is *awe, reverence, worship*. Jesus, as the demons well knew, was 'the Holy One of God' (Mk 1²⁴). In His life the holiness of God is translated into human terms. All who, in faith, accept His lordship are the 'holy ones', the 'saints' of the New Testament. They are those who are *separated for* God, dedicated to the doing of His will by what they say, what they do, and what they are. In them the Holy Spirit is at work. And just as the nature of holiness is to be seen in the life of Jesus, so the work of God through the Spirit is 'conforming believers' to the image of His Son—i.e. making them 'like Christ'. This is the end of the process—'when he appears we shall be like him' (1 Jn 3³, *RSV*).

Holiness is not one of the more popular qualities nowadays. It is thought to involve the pride of the 'holier than thou'; the narrowness which frowns on harmless pleasures; the splitting up of life into the 'holy' as opposed to the 'common'; the world over against the Church. The time is ripe for a new and serious study and proclamation of the scriptural idea of holiness. Let us see what our Epistles, and especially this passage, have to say.

(*1*) It is clear, from *vv.* 1 and 2, that the new life, to which the 'holy ones' are called, is a life of obedience; and from *vv.* 9 and 10 that it is obedience to 'the law of love' (cf. Jn 13³⁴, Rom 12⁸⁻¹⁰). Now Christ's 'new law' is very different from the old law, which was a series of written enactments to which precise obedience was possible and expected—something which a man strives to do in his own strength to gain merit before God. The new law is offer as well as demand, as the love which is demanded is the gift of the Spirit (Rom 5⁵). It is not the sort of law obedience to which commends a man to God, but the sort of life which results from the fact that a man *has been accepted by God*. In each concrete situation the believer is to present his body (Rom 12[1]) to God in such a way that it becomes the place where the love of God is shown forth.

There are two guides to the actual pattern of conduct involved—personal relation to God Himself (4[9]); and obedience to the 'instructions' (4[2]), i.e. the illustrations, based on the teaching of Christ, which show how love does in fact work out in various situations. Of course, Christian obedience is of a sort that does not take away the individual's responsibility to think.

Now this sort of life, though placed in prayer under the challenge of God's perfection (3[13], 5[23]), cannot in fact reach it—not only because the vessel can never hold all that God wills to give, but also because love, by its very nature, must always *'abound more and more'*. There is always a *pressing on* (Phil 3[12]), and perfection (Phil 3[15]) *is* in this pressing on. But we must be careful to avoid viewing holiness as a sort of inevitable spiritual progress, something not present at conversion but increasing gradually as time goes on. Sanctification is something involved in the *beginning* of the Christian life (4[7], 1 Cor 1[2], 6[11]). This 'model' church is very much at the beginning of the journey. The idea of inevitable progress carries with it terrible dangers of Pharisaism. It is better to think of holiness as a series of crises of response, beginning from conversion itself. At each crisis the believer submits himself to God and the instructions, with all the thought he can muster, but especially in humility and faith. He leaves 'spiritual progress' for God to take care of.

(2) Holiness, as we see from *vv.* 3 to 6, inevitably involves 'abstaining', discipline, control. There must be a sharp and recognizable difference between the conduct of 'saint' and 'sinner'. Paul takes up sex, as burning a problem to the Thessalonians as it is to us. The Christian is not sent into this explosive sphere of life and told to work out for himself 'the law of love'. There are *'charges'* (*v.* 2), based on the revealed truths of the faith. The body (if that is the *'vessel'* of *v.* 4) is not an unimportant casing of the immortal soul. The body is 'for the Lord', because 'bought with a price'; your bodies are 'members of Christ', 'temples of the Holy Ghost' (1 Cor 6[12–20]). Your body is not for selfish pleasure, but for God's glorification. And God is glorified in a life properly related to others in love. The sexual act, in particular, is not a trivial and unimportant

incident, but something fraught with inescapable relational consequences (1 Cor 6^{16}). When all this is understood, the question, 'Shall I then take from Christ his bodily parts and make them over to a harlot?' (1 Cor 6^{15}, *NEB*) has only to be asked to be answered. All sexual intercourse apart from God's ordination of holy matrimony must be considered in its aspect of wronging the brother (4^6)—or sister; spoiling somebody's marriage, if only our own. For marriage is only a holy glorification of God when it is a union 'in sanctification and honour' of bodies which, by the grace of God, have been *mastered*. We must be humble enough to receive Paul's negative teaching about marriage (1 Cor 7)—marriage as God's gracious provision to ensure that the seventh commandment is obeyed. We must also be humble enough to realize that we have not yet plumbed the depths of his positive teaching in Eph 5. We are especially called to work out today a new interpretation of the NT understanding of marriage in terms of God's own gift of the emancipation of woman. (In particular, what is our interpretation of the important word 'subordination'?) There is no frowning on innocent pleasures here. The whole aim of the scriptural idea of holiness is that the sphere of sex should blaze with glory.

(*3*) Even if we cannot interpret the word 'matter' in **4^6** as 'business', it is clear from verse 11 that business is very much involved in holiness. None of the activities of everyday is excluded from consideration. All are set in the context of obedience to the law of love. The Bishop of Woolwich was not the first to teach that holiness is 'worldly'!

(*4*) Over the life of holiness brood the three powerful realities of *vv*. 6 to 8. God's avenging, God's call, God's gift. God graciously warns His children of the consequences of disobeying the law of love—consequences best thought of as the missing of glory; He challenges to an exciting and satisfying adventure of 'body, soul, spirit', whole and healthy, used for the world; and He provides the means by which all these glorious prospects may become actual.

Holiness means being like Christ. The fact that it can be popularly thought of as proud, narrow, exclusive, life-denying (when He was the embodiment of love, humility, the friend of publicans and sinners, of the gluttonous and the winebibber, the carpenter) is a sign both of the failure of the Church's holiness and of the challenge of the Spirit to new dedication.

Holy Ghost, no more delay;
Come, and in Thy temple stay;
Now Thine inward witness bear,
Strong, and permanent, and clear;
Spring of life, Thyself impart,
Rise eternal in my heart. (MBH 568)

(2) 4¹³–5¹¹: The Christian Hope

(a) 4¹³⁻¹⁸: *No Hopeless Grief for the Dead!*

Summary: *The remedy for hopeless grief is contained within our Christian faith. Jesus died and rose again! Those who are His own share His victory. I have the Lord's authority for saying that, at the Coming, there will be no difference between dead and living. Both together will meet the returning Lord.*

The preaching and teaching at Thessalonica had been related to a series of three great events—the death of Christ, His resurrection, His coming. By faith in what God had done in the first two of these, the brethren had been brought into a new life characterized by waiting for the third. The Coming of Christ was believed to be 'near'; from which, not unnaturally, the conclusion was drawn that both Paul and the Thessalonian believers would live to experience it (see 2¹⁹, 4¹⁵). But Timothy brought news that, in the short period since Paul had left Thessalonica, some of the brethren had died. This fact involved an adjustment in the pattern of belief which the survivors were finding it difficult to make. They were troubled by doubts about the fate of those who had died. In particular, would they have a share in the joy of the Lord's Coming (still thought of as historically near)? Doubts had led to temptations to relapse into old forms of pre-conversion grief. Paul takes up this point.

4¹³. *'them that fall asleep'.* Paul uses a common euphemism for death, found in Greek writers from Homer onwards. The word does not, in itself, contain a 'gospel'; it is freely used by those who 'have no hope'. But, as in many other cases, the Christian faith gave the word 'a new lease of life'. The dead are those who 'fall asleep', because in Christ there *will be* an awakening.

'*that ye sorrow not, even as the rest*'. Some want to make this mean 'you may sorrow, so long as you do not sorrow as immoderately, or as hopelessly, as the rest'. But this strains the Greek word translated 'even as'. Paul does not exclude sorrow from the Christian life (cf. Rom 12¹⁵). He does, completely, exclude the hope-less sorrow of the non-Christian world.

'*the rest which have no hope*'. Paul has been taken to task for this. *Is* there '*no hope*' outside the Christian faith? What of the Greeks and the immortality of the soul; the mystery-religions with their doctrine of personal survival; the Pharisaic belief in resurrection? But we must remember that Paul the Pharisee had tested enough of the third of these to know that, in the light of the hope in Christ, their hope is 'no hope'.

4¹⁴. The Christian hope is anchored to the great 'salvation-events'. '*Jesus died and rose again.*' Paul puts the maximum flavour of hope into the language. It was '*Jesus*' who died— He who became *real man*, like us. And He '*died*'. Significantly, he does not say that Jesus 'fell asleep'. He uses a word for death in its starkest form. His death was *real* death; but more, it was the 'death of death'—something which makes the death of believers in Him *truly* a 'falling asleep'. And Jesus, who thus died, '*rose again*'.

This we believe. The 'if' implies no doubt; it draws a conclusion from what is certainly accepted. 'Since we believe' (*RSV*)—what follows? The *RSV* translates 'even so, through Jesus, God will bring with him those who have fallen asleep'. Comparison with the *RV* translation reveals the problem. Do the words, literally translated in *RSV* 'through Jesus', go with '*fallen asleep*' (*RV*) or with 'will bring' (*RSV*)? We have to decide which of the two stresses Paul is more likely, in this context, to have made. Does he stress that God's bringing '*with him*' of those '*that are fallen asleep*' is to be through the instrumentality of Jesus; or that those who are so brought are, not the dead in general, but those who have fallen asleep through Jesus? On the whole, the latter is to be preferred (so also *NEB*). 'God will bring through Christ with him' is an overloaded expression; the 'instrumentality of Jesus' is safe-guarded in the description which follows. The connection of '*through Jesus*' with '*falling asleep*' seems to be demanded by a gap in the argument. *Why* does it follow from His death and resurrection that God will bring 'with him' '*them . . . that are fallen asleep*'? Only because they, by faith (as later Pauline letters will show), have made that death and resurrection their own—i.e. they are 'in Christ'. It must, however, be admitted that 'falling asleep *through* Jesus' is a difficult phrase for the more usual 'dead *in* Christ' (*v.* 16). It must be an expression of the truth that 'if we die we die to the Lord' (Rom 14[8]). Jesus is 'Lord of both the dead and the living' (Rom 14[9]). The dying of the believer is 'through Him', i.e. in His hands.

4[15]. '. . . *we that are alive, that are left unto the coming . . .*' The Coming is 'near'. But what does 'nearness' mean? The naïve interpretation is that it means 'about to *happen*'. Circumstances were to modify this interpretation, but here Paul adheres to it, and puts himself with the Thessalonian survivors as those who will be alive at the Coming.

'*we . . . shall in no wise precede*'. The bereaved community had fixed on this main point of anxiety—are we to experience the Coming, while our loved ones are left behind? '*In no wise*', says Paul, giving as his authority '*the word of the Lord*'. If this means a word spoken by the historical Jesus, it must be one (like Acts 20[35]) which has not survived in the Gospel tradition, for none of the sayings which resemble this (e.g. Mt 16[27], 24[30]) really cover the point at issue. Jesus did, of course, speak of the possible death of his followers (Mk 10[39], 13[12]; Mt 10[28]; Jn 16[2]) and He *might* have spoken of their part in the 'coming of the Son of Man'. But if so, it is odd that it did not survive in the Gospel tradition, as it would have been of great interest and relevance to the communities which preserved and collected the sayings. It seems, therefore, more likely that we have to do here with a word of the Exalted Lord, communicated through a prophet, or through the teaching tradition.

4[16]. What is not clear is whether 'the word of the Lord' referred to in **4[15]** is being cited in this verse and the next. It seems probable that it is. The Parousia is described in apocalyptic imagery. But Paul is not interested in the imagery for its own sake. He is severely practical, and selects from the apocalyptic scenario only those touches which are relevant to the point he is discussing, i.e. the part to be played at the Parousia by those who have 'fallen asleep in Jesus'. The points he selects are these:

(*a*) '*The Lord himself shall descend from heaven*'—the Lord and none other.

(*b*) There follow three sounds—'*a shout*' (the Greek shows that this is an authoritative word of command); '*the voice of the archangel*' (we are not told his name); and '*the trump of God*' (a time-honoured apocalyptic symbol; cf. Ex 19[16, 19]; Zech 9[14]; Mt 24[31]; 1 Cor 15[52]). It is useless to speculate about the precise nature and inter-relation of these sounds. The context suggests the authoritative command of God, directed to 'raising the dead'.

(*c*) The next part of the unfolding drama of the End is the rising of the dead—'*first*'—before

4[17]. (*d*) the rapture of the living (presumably with the trans-formed bodies to be described later in 1 Cor 15[51-7]) '*to meet the Lord in the air*'. '*together with them*' is an incidental (and affirmative) answer to the question of so many, 'Shall I see my loved ones again'? For Paul this is a much less important point than 'meeting the Lord'! Once this meeting has taken place there will be no more partings: we shall be '*ever . . . with the Lord*'. It is tantalizing to be left in the air in this way. It is impossible not to ask, 'What happens next?' *The Lord and His Church* do not, presumably, remain in the air. Do they, after the meeting, return to heaven? Or do they continue to earth, presumably for the conflict with Antichrist and the Last Judgement? If we must take a choice between these two, the latter seems much more likely. The word for 'meeting' is that used in Acts 28[15]—'the brethren' (from Rome) 'came to meet us'—of course, to escort us on to Rome. Similarly, the believ-ers, dead and living, meet the returning Christ, to escort Him to earth. If so, being '*with the Lord*' will involve being as-sociated with Him in all His subsequent acts. But it is better not to speculate. Only that much has been revealed which meets the situation—no hopeless grief for the dead. They died through Jesus; they remain in Him; they will not be left behind, when God decrees the End; they will be brought with Jesus; they, with us, will meet Him and remain with Him for ever.

4[18]. The doubt and sorrow of the bereaved had affected the whole community. Pagan sorrow must go. But there is Christian comfort to take its place—a comfort which it is the pastoral responsibility of all to administer. As Augustine says, 'Let sorrow cease in the face of such consolation'.

Note 10: Death

Every preacher, indeed every Christian, must be able to administer comfort from God's word 'concerning them that fall asleep'; to show, as much amid the restraint and stoicism of the West as amid the emotional demonstrations of such a country as India, that the Christian faith excludes hopeless grief. This can only be done by preaching (*a*) our death (*b*) His death (*c*) our death in Him.

(*a*) What is death? What does the Bible mean by 'death' in such a verse, for example, as Rom 5^{12}—'Therefore, as through one man sin entered into the world, and death through sin ...'? On this verse Professor Dodd (*Moffatt Commentary*, 81) writes: 'Obviously we cannot accept such a speculation as an account of the origin of death, which is a natural process inseparable from organic existence in the world we know, and devoid of any moral significance.' Does the Bible mean that death 'as a natural process'is caused by sin? Or is there some other meaning? Let us, in faith, look for a moment at the passage to which Rom 5^{12} refers—Gen 2^{4b}–3^{24}; in faith, that is, that the passage is not simply an ancient fable, but a vehicle for the revelation of God's truth. Does the account of the creation in *Genesis* throw light on the meaning of 'death'? If it intended to say that death '*as a natural process*' is the penalty of man's sin, we should expect that it would represent Adam and Eve as created immortal in such a way that if they had not sinned they would not have died. Does the passage *say* this? Gen 3^{22} says No. Only if man should eat of the tree of life, would he live for ever. But do not Gen 2^{17} and 3^{19} give us pause? 2^{17} threatens death as the penalty for disobedience to God's command not to eat of the tree of the knowledge of good and evil. 3^{19} looks as if it is the carrying out of this threat—'In the sweat of thy face shalt thou eat bread, till thou return unto the ground; for out of it wast thou taken; for dust thou art and unto dust shalt thou return.' But let us look more closely. What is threatened in 2^{17} is instant death (in the day that you eat of it you shall die). But this is not what is carried out in 3^{19}, which surely states a *fact* about man, rather than carrying out a sentence. Man is of the ground, the dust, and to the dust he shall return, which is exactly what Paul says of Adam in 1 Cor 15⁴⁷ (*RSV*)—the 'first man was from the earth, a man of dust'. The *Genesis* passage sets before us man created mortal, with, in 3²², the glittering prospect of immortality. Man's disobedience then deprived man of an immortality he might have obtained. But it did more; it put a new meaning into the word 'death'. And this is what the passage, duly demythologized (!), reveals. When the Bible speaks of death it means death not as a natural process, but as the terrible thing it has become for sinful man without God. There is nothing sentimental about the biblical view of death. It is 'the King of terrors' (Job 18¹⁴); something to the fear of which men live all their lives in bondage (see Heb 2¹⁵). The bearing of Jesus facing death in Gethsemane (so different from the heroism of the martyr or the calm of Socrates) is His tasting, as true man, this elemental human terror of death. And because man is a sinner, not only in his body but in his total being, the death contemplated in the Bible is 'total death', the death of the whole personality. The Bible never evades the issue with the doctrine of a naturally immortal soul which cannot die. Its doctrine, both of sin and death, is much more radical than that.

(*b*) First the diagnosis; then the cure. Jesus died and rose again—'who abolished death' (2 Tim 1¹⁰) by bringing to nought 'him that had the power of death, that is, the devil' (Heb 2¹⁴).

> *It was a strange and dreadful strife*
> *When life and death contended.*
> *The victory remained with life.* (*MHB* 210)

God was active in Christ's death (2 Cor 5¹⁹); 'Him who knew no sin he made to be sin on our behalf' (2 Cor 5²¹), 'a curse for us' (Gal 3¹³). Death, the judgement of God on sin, fell now on the sinless One—and sin itself was judged. Here, at last, is a death which is not the penalty for sin—and from it flows life, 'because it was not possible that he should be holden of it' (Acts 2²⁴). The second Adam won the immortality which the first Adam had failed to obtain. And 'Christ being raised from the dead dieth no more' (Rom 6⁹).

(*c*) So there is a Person—a living Person—whose death was not defeat but victory; victory which faith sees as ultimately final victory (1 Cor 15²⁶). And to that Person we may be joined in faith, and so share His victory. Baptism, inseparable

F

from faith, is said by Paul to be a sharing in His death (see Rom 6³⁻⁷) and an entry into the sphere of His life (Rom 6⁵⁻⁸, Col 2¹²). This is nothing magical. The new life of faith is a life in the spirit; the life of those who reckon themselves 'to be dead unto sin, but alive unto God in Christ Jesus' (Rom 6¹¹); who continually 'put to death the deeds of the body' (Rom 8¹³, *RSV*); who 'no longer live unto themselves, but unto him who for their sakes died and rose again' (2 Cor 5¹⁵). And because the new life of faith is a life 'unto him', it is the doing of His will and the bearing of 'the fellowship of his sufferings' (Phil 3¹⁰)—paradoxically enough a life which Paul calls a 'bearing about in the body the dying of Jesus' (2 Cor 4¹⁰).

In the time between the Resurrection and the End, death as a physical fact has still to be undergone. But, for those who are united by faith to Christ, death has lost its sting (1 Cor 15⁵⁵). In the faith-encounter with the living Christ they have already 'passed out of death into life' (Jn 5²⁴, cf. 1 Jn 3¹⁴; *OEE* 57, *GPL* 85). Physical death has become a relatively unimportant incident.

This, then, is the comfort of the Christian hope. Those '*that are fallen asleep in Jesus*' (4¹⁴) are 'the dead in Christ' (4¹⁶). Because of His death and resurrection, because we and they have in faith partaken in that death and resurrection, we can have absolute confidence that we, with them, shall meet Him in the future.

The problem of the 'intermediate state' is bound to arise. But there are some serious questions to which the Bible does not give an answer. The dead in this passage are clearly 'asleep' when the last trumpet sounds. Should we think of the dead in the timelessness of sleep, in what appears to us to be the interval between their death and the End? Or when, in 2 Cor 5⁸ and Phil 1²³, Paul speaks of death as gain, because it will mean 'being with' or 'at home with' Christ, does he go beyond the idea of 'sleep' to that of a provisional judgement taking place at death? We cannot be sure. What we know is sufficient. The dead in Christ are 'with Him'.

> *When He comes, our glorious King,*
> *All His ransomed home to bring,*
> *Then anew this song we'll sing:*
> *Hallelujah! what a Saviour!* (*MBH* 176)

With joy like His shall every saint
His vacant tomb survey;
Then rise with his ascending Lord
To realms of endless day. (*MHB* 217)

(b) 5¹⁻¹¹: *Keep Awake and Be Sober!*

Summary: *There is no answer to 'When?'—for He comes with-out warning. His coming will be terrible for those in darkness. But you are in the light! Let us then live as befits those who are in the light, awake and sober, fighting the fight of faith. This we can do, because of what He has done, and will do, for us.*

In the crisis sparked off by the death of some Thessalonian brethren, many questions were being asked about the Coming. In particular, the perennial question, 'When?' In this section Paul gives the only possible Christian answer.

5¹. *'times' and 'seasons'.* The two Greek words here used are sometimes synonyms. But essentially there is a difference. The first is 'man's time', 'clock time', on-going time measured in days, hours, minutes. The second is a stretch of clock-time filled with content, opportunity, fulfilment; and so, often, 'God's time' (e.g. Mk 1¹⁵; 2 Thess 2⁶). The Thessalonians were asking, 'How long must we wait?' and 'Through what historical crises will God decree the End?' Paul begins his answer by telling them that they need not have asked the question.

5². If they had only reminded themselves of the teaching they had received, they would know that the Coming cannot be assigned beforehand to a point in time at all. Its symbol is the symbol given by Jesus—the 'thief' (Mt 24⁴³; see *AMW* 141). The Coming is here the *'day of the Lord'*. This is a dominating concept of OT prophecy, from Amos onwards (Amos 5¹⁸, ²⁰). It is the day God will choose to complete His work in the world. It is a day of cosmic catastrophe and the terrors of judgement— and, less frequently, the glories of salvation. In the NT the *'day of the Lord'* is 'the day of Jesus Christ' (Phil 1⁶), and much of the OT imagery is transferred bodily to the Coming of Christ' (see *KG* 84).

5³. The thief comes when you least expect him. So does

Christ on 'that day'. Luke 17²⁷ gives the typical judgement situation. When everybody is saying, 'All's well! Nothing to fear!'—the Day is there! And to the unprepared it comes as the very opposite of salvation—'*destruction*'. It is compared to birth-pangs, coming suddenly, and initiating a time of pain and birth which cannot then be avoided.

5⁴. Now Paul speaks as a pastor, the 'mother' and 'father' (2⁷⁻¹¹) of the '*brethren*'. They included (we know from *v.* 14 below) some who were 'fainthearted'. Perhaps these, perhaps others, were afraid of the terrors of the 'day of the Lord'. So Paul expounds the fundamental difference between the OT 'day of the Lord' and the 'day of Christ'. He had set the scene by saying that the Day comes '*as a thief in the night*' (5²). Most of the terror of that situation comes from the darkness. The thief who comes in daylight is a very different proposition. '*But ye . . . are not in darkness.*' The One who is to come is the One who has already 'delivered us out of the power of darkness' (Col 1¹³), so that the Day which, for the unprepared, is destruction, is, for you, something very different.

5⁵. The stress is on '*all*'. All, the fainthearted included, are '*sons of light*', '*sons of the day*'. This is a Hebrew expression. A man is said to be the 'son of' that which essentially characterizes him. 'Night and darkness', 'light and day' have now become moral and spiritual realities. By faith in Christ, the Light of the World, you have become '*sons of light, and sons of the day*'. Only those need fear that Day who continue to be sons of night and of darkness.

5⁶. Now comes the authentic Pauline ethical exhortation, aptly described as '*Be* what you are!' This is the ethics of 'therefore', of 'the Imperative which follows the Indicative'. You *are* (praise God!), by grace through faith, sons of light. (And so are we, who write this letter.) *Therefore*—let us be what we are! '*Let us not sleep*' (as the disciples did in Gethsemane, as the world does), but '*let us watch*' (keep morally and spiritually alert and ready) and '*be sober*' (not only physically but morally and spiritually free from all that leads to over-excitement, insensibility, lack of control).

5⁷. Night is the time for sleep and intoxication.

5⁸. But we have come into the new day, with its imperious demand for sobriety. We must '*be sober*' because this is a time of crisis and danger, when we must fight against evil (2 Thess 2⁷; 1 Pet 5⁸). The military metaphor, more fully worked out in Rom 13¹¹⁻¹⁴ and Eph 6¹⁰, goes back to Isa 59¹⁷. The weapons are defensive—the protection of head and heart. And they are the familiar triad of faith, love and hope (cf. **1³**). Where these are living and active, the devil has no power.

5⁹⁻¹⁰. Here are the reasons why we may indeed wear the 'hope of salvation' as our 'helmet' in the warfare of the Christian life (*v*. 8). Our salvation rests not upon our own efforts, but on God's initiative. Through Jesus Christ, God has set us in the way of salvation. God does not do everything; the '*obtaining of salvation*' is something active, involving faith. But God has done His part!

5¹⁰. And we can do ours—because Christ '*died for us*'. There is not much about the Atonement in these Epistles, but the almost casual way in which Christ's atoning death is mentioned here shows that it was there in the preaching and teaching, only not taken up in detail because there were other points which needed treatment. And Christ who died, *lives*, so that we may hope to '*live together with him*'. 'Waking' and 'sleeping' in this verse are used in the sense of 'living' or 'being dead', and look back to **4¹⁵**.

5¹¹. This section, like the one before it (**4¹⁸**) contains material for use in mutual pastoral concern—for 'exhorting' (encouraging, strengthening) and 'building up'. The Messiah *builds* His Church (Mt 16¹⁸), a 'spiritual building' (1 Pet 2⁵). But His building is done through the mutual love and care by which each 'builds up' the other. Again Paul tempers his demand with praise. You are doing this—go on doing it.

Note 11: Night and Day

Here is the authentic preaching of the Coming.

The Christian life is an adventure. You never know what is going to happen next! In particular you must take account of the 'Day of the Lord', just as much as you must take account of your own death. There is no knowing when the time will be.

The Day of the Lord is like a thief in the night. It comes when you least expect it. Be prepared!

But your life lies between two crises, and the Day of the Lord is the lesser of the two. The Lord who *will* come is the Lord who *has* come. His death cut history in two; and faith in Him crucified has similarly cut your life into two. You have already come from the dark into the day. Being prepared, for you, is not a matter of looking anxiously into the future, but, first and foremost, thankfully into the past.

And the Lord who came and will come is the Lord who comes now, in challenge and grace. The preparation for which He calls is that faith about the past, and that hope for the future, concentrated into readiness for obedient and faithful action, here and now.

Our preaching from this passage will reflect the contrast. *Night*—darkness, sleep, drunkenness, wrath; and *Day*—light, waking up, being sober, fighting, fellowship, salvation.

It was night when Judas went from the upper room to betray Jesus (Jn 13³⁰). Though the light had come into the world, he loved darkness rather than light (see Jn 3¹⁹). The whole symbolism of light and darkness is brought into the gospel. God is light (1 Jn 1⁵); over against Him is the power of darkness (Col 1¹³), whose sign is hatred (1 Jn 2¹¹), sin, evil, falsehoood (1 Jn 1⁵⁻⁷; *GPL* 20 f, 23 f). Those who 'sit in darkness' (Mt 4¹⁶) do not know where they are going (Jn 12³⁵). They sleep, between the deception of dreams and unconsciousness, unready, like the disciples in Gethsemane, for action (Mk 14³⁷). They get drunk, like the servants in the parables (Mt 24²⁹, Lk 12⁴⁵), not knowing that the Master will come. All this is not a superior description of someone else, but a stirring call to reality. Judas was a disciple; so were those who slept in Gethsemane. There is darkness all around!

But the true believer is one who has responded to the call, 'Awake, thou that sleepest and arise from the dead, and Christ shall shine upon thee' (Eph 5¹⁴). He knows that with Christ the Light has come, the day has dawned. The rising bell has sounded. It is time to get up and dress! The dress is battle-dress for the Christian conflict—God's gift of faith, love and the sure hope of salvation. He is to be what the disciples in Gethsemane were not—*awake*—his readiness for the Lord who comes at the End revealed in his readiness for obedience here and now. Over against the intoxication of those in darkness,

he is to be *sober*—a sobriety 'filled with the Spirit' (Eph 5[18]),
and revealing itself in service (2 Tim 4[5]), prayer (1 Pet 4[7]), love
(1 Pet 4[8]) and hard fighting (5[8]).

(3) 5[12–24]: More about the Upbuilding of the Church

'Build one another up', Paul has said, 'just as you are doing.'
He now begins to bring the letter to a close with some very
practical injunctions to show what 'building-up' involves. He
speaks (*a*) about honouring leaders (*vv.* 12–13), (*b*) about
pastoral responsibilities incumbent on all (*v.* 14), (*c*) about
fundamental principles of the Christian life (*vv.* 15–18), (*d*)
about spiritual gifts (*vv.* 19–22) and (*e*) closes the section with a
prayer and a word of encouragement (*vv.* 23–24).

(a) 5[12–13]: *Honour your Leaders*
5[12–13a]. The early Church had a ministry from the beginning
(Eph 4[7–16]). In Acts 14[23] we read that, at the end of the first
missionary journey, Paul and Barnabas 'appointed . . . elders
in every church'. But it is clear from 1 Cor 12 that such appointment was the result, not of mere human choice, but of the
working of the Spirit. In the community of the Spirit-filled,
the gifts of the Spirit were divided 'to each one severally' (1
Cor 12[11]). Among the gifts of the Spirit were 'helps' and
'governments' (1 Cor 12[28]), i.e. helpers, administrators (*RSV*).
The ministry of the Church was constituted as the communities
discerned and accepted the Spirit's working. So here Paul begs
the brethren to realize that some among them do three things—
'*labour*' (work hard at the Lord's work), '*are over*' them (take
the lead), and '*admonish*' (counsel, with special reference to the
pointing out and setting right of wrongs). Paul asks that these
activities should be acknowledged as gifts of the Spirit, and
that these individuals should be 'known' (recognized as God-
given Church leaders), and esteemed '*exceedingly highly*' with
a willing heart ('*in love*'). But we must note that the leaders
are to be esteemed '*for their work*', and not for their status!

5[13b]. This apparently general injunction is attached to the
section about honouring leaders—and may belong to it. It may
well be that tension had attended the growth of leadership.
Perhaps the admonishing had been resented, or the naturally
equalitarian Greek community had been jealous of the gifts of

government given to some. Paul pleads for peace and the mutual harmony which comes to the body of Christ when 'bonded and knit together by every constituent joint, the whole frame grows through the due activity of each part, and builds itself up in love' (Eph 4¹⁶, *NEB*; see *HKM* 115).

(b) 5¹⁴: *Pastoral Responsibilities Incumbent on All*

Some have thought that Paul now turns from the community as a whole, and addresses specifically the leaders of *vv.* 12 and 13. But it is impossible to make a distinction between the same word '*brethren*' in *v.* 12 and *v.* 14. Paul still addresses the community as a whole. In providing leaders, the Holy Spirit does not give them an absolute monopoly of pastoral functions. The image of the Church where the leaders do all the work and the congregation remains passive is fundamentally un-biblical. In the Thessalonian Church were to be found the '*disorderly*', the '*faint-hearted*' and the '*weak*'. '*Disorderly*' is a military term, used of a soldier out of line, out of step. In these Epistles, (especially 2 Thess 3⁶⁻¹⁵), it seems to be used of those who 'work not at all' (2 Thess 3¹¹; cf. 4¹¹)—the loafers. '*the fainthearted*' may be those who have doubts about the fate of the dead, and fears about the Coming (4¹³–5¹¹). '*the weak*' may have been specially subject to sexual temptations (4¹⁻⁸). But we must not try to be too specific. All the brethren have the responsibility of pointing out the faults of the disorderly and setting them right, encouraging the fainthearted, and helping the weak. But, Paul adds, Christian pastoral responsibility in these, as in all other cases, can only be fulfilled if there is God-given patience.

(c) 5¹⁵⁻¹⁸: *Fundamental Principles of the Christian Life*

5¹⁵. 'Ye have heard that it was said, An eye for an eye and a tooth for a tooth' (Mt 5³⁸, cf. Ex 21²³⁻⁵, Deut 19²¹, Lev 24¹⁹⁻²⁰). It is, of course, important to recognize that this *lex talionis* represents a significant moral advance on the demand of Lamech, 'the natural man', to be avenged seventy-seven fold (Gen 4²⁴). The OT points, in many passages, still further away from the desire for revenge (e.g. Ex 23⁴, Ps 7⁴⁻⁵, Prov 25²¹⁻², Job 31²⁹). But Jesus abolished the law of revenge entirely, and this 'high ethic' the NT consistently proclaims (e.g. 1 Cor 4¹²⁻¹³, 6⁷⁻⁸, 1 Pet 2¹⁹⁻²¹, Rom 12¹⁷⁻²¹). A comparison with 3¹¹ shows that 'good' and 'bad' are to be defined always with reference to action inspired by, or contrary to, 'love'. And the loving service a Christian is to show to his Christian brother is exactly the loving service he is to show to his non-Christian friend.

5¹⁶. If a man is reconciled to God, he is in touch with the source of perennial joy (Ps 16¹¹), a joy which no adverse human circumstances can destroy—cf. Acts 5⁴¹, 16²⁵, Phil 4⁴⁻⁵ (written from prison), Rom 5³⁻⁴, Col 1²⁴, 1 Pet 4¹³.

5¹⁷. If a man has been 'apprehended by Christ', his whole life will be that response which is essential prayer—both the response of conscious communion with God and the wider response of service.

5¹⁸. The man who can say 'Thanks be to God for his gift beyond words' (2 Cor 9¹⁵, *NEB*) has a cause for thanksgiving which can be used on any occasion, however much it may seem to contradict the goodness of God. We are in the presence of a supernatural ethic, impossible to unaided man. But in Christ God has fulfilled His will to come to man's aid. In the power of the Spirit the impossible becomes possible.

N.B. For more about **5¹⁷, 5¹⁸** see *Note* 8. For **5¹²⁻¹⁴** see also *Note* 3.

(d) 5¹⁹⁻²²: *Spiritual Gifts*

5¹⁹⁻²⁰. We are here in a context which 1 Cor 12–14 depicts much more fully. The early Church lived in an intense experience of the powerful working of the Spirit. But the Spirit was not given in undifferentiated power, enabling every Christian to do everything. As 1 Cor 12⁴⁻¹¹ shows, when the Holy Spirit came upon a community of believers, His presence was made known in the endowment of different individuals with different 'gifts'. Paul makes a list of these. There are 'intellectual' gifts, such as wisdom, knowledge, discernment; gifts of speaking, whether in the intelligible utterances of prophecy or the ecstatic voice of 'tongues'; or there would be gifts to some of action—e.g. the performance of miracles of healing. But Paul found it necessary, especially in 1 Cor 12¹⁻³, to issue a strong warning. The Holy Spirit is not the only spiritual agency at work in the world! There are evil spiritual agencies who, as well as the Holy Spirit, can take control of, and work through, human faculties. Enthusiastic or ecstatic phenomena might appear in the heathen temple as well as in the Christian congregation. Outward appearances might not differ so very much. So Christians need a 'test' to help them to distinguish between the working of the Holy Spirit and other powers (1 Cor 12³). They similarly need regulative principles (1 Cor 12⁷, 14³). One of the Holy Spirit's own gifts is 'the ability to distinguish true spirits from false' (1 Cor 12¹⁰, *NEB*). If the five short, sharp commands of this section are to be seen against a background such as this, they seem to be a closely bound unity, all dealing with the one theme of 'spiritual' phenomena.

Paul had heard of a tendency in Thessalonica to suppress spiritual manifestations. (Did this come from the leaders, over-zealous for orderliness?) This tendency must be curbed. On the one hand the Spirit (thought of in His aspect of 'fire'—Acts 2³, Rom 12¹¹), must not be quenched, and prophecy (the powerful, convincing proclamation of the word of God—see especially 1 Cor 14) must not be despised.

5²¹⁻². *'Prove all things; hold fast that which is good.'* This is a familiar, well-loved phrase. If it is the correct translation of the Greek, Paul has now left the subject of spiritual gifts and is giving general ethical maxims. But it is much more likely that the theme is still the same, as *RSV* and *NEB* interpret. *NEB* translates (5¹⁹⁻²²) 'Do not stifle inspiration, and do not despise prophetic utterances, but bring them all to the test and then keep what is good in them and avoid the bad of whatever kind.' 1 Cor 12³ and 1 Jn 4¹⁻³ throw light on the background. In the first of these Paul takes the phrase 'A curse on Jesus!' (*NEB*). (Whether this sort of thing was actually said by a Jew on the basis of Deut 21²³, or whether Paul takes the most extreme and shocking example he can think of, is not clear.) His point is that no matter how ecstatic or 'spiritual' the phenomena may be, nobody who says 'A curse on Jesus' can possibly be speaking 'by the Holy Spirit' (of course because it is the work of the Spirit to 'glorify Jesus'—Jn 16¹⁴). Similarly in 1 Jn 4¹⁻³, schismatics with a false Christology claim the Spirit, and their claim has to be tested by the same fundamental standard (*GPL* 93 f). Many think that behind the words 'prove' and 'hold fast' lies a reminiscence of an unwritten saying of Jesus—'Be approved bankers, or money changers, or testers of coin.' This may well be a genuine saying, and the idea of 'assaying' the coin, sticking to the true metal and rejecting the base, would be quite appropriate. It is no doubt regrettable to give up the familiar generality of the *RV* translation, but its truth is really contained in *v.* 15.

(e) 5²³⁻⁴: *A Prayer and a Word of Encouragement*
Now follows, most appropriately, a prayer which gathers together all the demands and aspirations of the second part of the letter. Paul has asked for purity, for hard and quiet work, for hope in bereavement, for watchfulness and sobriety, for mutual upbuilding to the heights of the Christian life. But all this is empty dreaming, apart from the act of God.

5²³. So he prays to '*the God of peace himself*' (cf. Rom 15³³, 1 Cor 14³³); i.e. the God who gives the gift of final blessedness, which is communion with Himself—a gift on which peaceful relations with others (5¹³) and peace of mind (Rom 15¹³) depend. The prayer is for 'entire sanctification'—may He '*sanctify you wholly*'. The language is OT, 'be ye holy; for I am holy' (Lev 11⁴⁴). But the process of sanctification is something God does—'I am the Lord which sanctify you' (Ex 31¹³). To be sanctified, then, is to receive a share in the most fundamental characteristic of God Himself. God in Christ 'called' the Thessalonian believers 'in sanctification' (4⁷), 'in sanctification of the Spirit' (2 Thess 2¹³). That is, through their response to the call of God in Christ, and through their reception of the gift of the Spirit, they were set aside for God; received, with all their imperfections, into communion with Him. Paul's prayer is that God will not cease from His activity in the lives of the believers until His gift of Himself has conquered their sins and inadequacies; until they are, in fact, what they became, in intention, at their conversion. God's intention is *wholeness*. The whole personality of the believers is to be preserved without loss and without stain for presentation to Christ at His coming. '. . . *spirit and soul and body*'. Paul is not writing a treatise on psychology, and it is foolish to argue from this verse that Paul thought of the human personality as divided into three parts. There are other components of man, e.g. heart and mind. But all these terms really refer to the whole human personality in one of its aspects—a thinking being, a feeling or willing being, etc. So here Paul is describing the personality in its fulness. '*spirit*' can hardly here mean 'that portion of the

Holy Spirit received by the believer'. It is the human spirit (cf. 1 Cor 2^{11}), i.e. man in his capacity as creature of God, intended for communion with Him. The *'soul'* is man as a living being. Essentially, Paul adheres to the OT notion of man as 'embodied spirit' or 'animated body'. Note that, in contrast to Greek notions of body as the unimportant casing of the immortal soul, here 'body' is 'for eternity', an essential aspect of the personality.

> *Didst Thou not die that I might live*
> *No longer to myself, but Thee,*
> *Might body, soul and spirit give*
> *To Him who gave Himself for me?*
> *Come then, my Master and my God,*
> *Take the dear purchase of Thy blood.* (*MHB* 558)

5^{24}. Paul's prayer may seem far too bold for the Thessalonians with their disorderly, faint-hearted, weak members, and so much 'lacking in their faith' (3^{10}). But the thing for which Paul prays is not a human possibility but an act of God. Their eyes are turned from themselves to God's faithfulness. 'Of one thing I am certain: the One who started the good work in you will bring it to completion by the Day of Christ Jesus' (Phil 1^6, *NEB*; *KG* 83–4).

> *The most impossible of all*
> *Is, that I e'er from sin should cease;*
> *Yet shall it be, I know it shall;*
> *Jesus, look to Thy faithfulness!*
> *If nothing is too hard for Thee,*
> *All things are possible to me.* (*MHB* 548)

N.B. For 5^{23-4}, see also *Notes* 1 and 19.

Note 12: Edification

'I will build my church', said Jesus (Mt 16^{18}). The temple at Jerusalem will be destroyed (Mk 13^{1-2}). In its place the Risen Christ (Jn 2^{19}) will raise up the temple of the New Age, a 'spiritual house' in which believers are 'living stones' (1 Pet 2^5). Jesus is not only the builder, but the 'foundation' (1 Cor 3^{11}) and the 'chief corner stone' (Eph 2^{20}). *Edification* is the continuous process by which Christ's Church is built up, or (the metaphor sometimes gets mixed) grows up 'into him which is the head' (Eph 4$^{13-16}$).

Christ builds up His Church through apostles (1 Cor 3^{10}), and prophets (i.e. *preachers*). An important text for us here is 1 Cor 14^3—'But he that prophesieth speaketh unto men edification, and comfort, and consolation.' But 'edification' is not only the work of ministers and preachers, but of every believer. '*Build each other up*', Paul had said in 5^{11}. The passage 5$^{11-22}$ sets before us, for judgement and challenge, the picture of a church 'being built up'.

At the heart of such a church are two fundamental realities: the activity of God (the gift of the Spirit—*vv*. 19–22); and that whole attitude of obedient receptiveness described as 'praying without ceasing' (*v*. 17). God's gifts, given and received, crystallize into relationships of reconciliation ('Be at peace among yourselves'); and the activities of edification, the responsibility *both* of those who, in the Lord, are 'over' the others (*v*. 12) *and* of *all* the believers (*v*. 14). These 'upbuilding' activities are directed not only to the 'disorderly', the 'fainthearted', the 'weak', but to all. They consist in 'admonishing', 'encouraging' and 'supporting'. All are patiently to care for each, each for all (*v*. 14). Immediate perfection is not expected. There will be '*evil*' (*v*. 15)—not only from without but from within. But evil is to be overcome by 'a following after that which is good', directed not only to one another but to all (*v*. 15). In a community in such a process of edification there will be 'constant joy' (*v*. 16) and 'constant thanksgiving' (*v*. 18). This picture of edification bears out what is more specifically stated in other places—that the upbuilding of the Church is not an end in itself. The spiritual house which is the Church exists to be the place of God's presence (Eph 2^{22}), and the giving out of His truth to the world (1 Pet 2$^{4-10}$).

A prime need for the preacher today is to recapture the biblical idea of edification as the main aim of his task. Edification is usually connected with the private life of an individual. *The Concise Oxford Dictionary* defines 'edify' as 'benefit spiritually'. If we ever use the language of edifying and being edified these days this surely is what we mean. We hear 'a good sermon' and are spiritually benefited. But as individuals. In the NT, however, edification is *always* a matter of fellowship. It is that activity by which Christ so shapes His living stones that they can fit together into that community which shows forth God to the world. The preacher should direct his work to this end.

And if edification can be saved from individualism, it may go on to be saved from denominationalism. No doubt the first efforts should be directed to the building up of congregations. But we must not stop there. A novel kind of ministry is required which will begin, under Christ, to build up denominations into the spiritual house which is the Church of Christ. No scheme of Reunion has much chance of success without this ministry. Let us pray, in readiness to be the answer to our prayers, for the time described in Acts 9³¹, where 'the church . . . had peace, being edified; and, walking in the fear of the Lord and in the comfort of the Holy Spirit, was multiplied'.

> *He bids us build each other up;*
> *And, gathered into one,*
> *To our high calling's glorious hope*
> *We hand in hand go on.* (*MHB* 745)

5²⁵⁻⁸: Conclusion

5²⁵. Paul has prayed for the Thessalonians. He now humbly asks for their prayers for himself and his companions (cf. 2 Thess 3¹, Rom 15³⁰, Eph 6¹⁸⁻¹⁹, Col 4³).

5²⁶. Here we see Paul's fatherly love for all the members of the church. All are to be greeted with the symbol of Christian love —the holy kiss. In the early Church this symbol was a kiss on the cheek. The 'kiss of peace' has been preserved in various forms in the churches of East and West, and has come into the liturgy of the Church of South India. Here the 'kiss of peace' or simply 'the Peace' is given at the beginning of the final part of the service (the Breaking of the Bread). It may be of interest to quote the official instructions. 'When the Peace is given, the giver places his right palm against the right palm of the receiver, and each closes his left hand over the other's right hand. The Peace is given before the Offertory (see Mt 5²³, ²⁴) as a sign of fellowship, and the offertory sentences (i.e. Ps 133¹, 1 Cor 10¹⁷, Ps 27¹⁷) recall Augustine's teaching that the sacrifice we offer is our unity in Christ. The presbyter gives the Peace to those ministering with him, and these in turn give it to the congregation. It may be passed through the congregation either along the rows, or from those in front to those behind. Each person, as he gives the Peace, may say in a low voice "The Peace of God" or "The Peace of God be with you".'

5²⁷. Now Paul's love for the church comes to a surprising expression. He writes in the first person; no doubt a sign that at this point he is writing the conclusion of the letter, as was his custom (cf. Gal 6¹¹), with his own hand. He uses the very strong language of 'adjuring them by the Lord' that the Epistle be read to *all* the brethren. Does he refer to reading the letter at the assembly for public worship, and is the strength of the language needed to start a new custom? Does he refer to a difficult task of seeking some out in their homes? Is he afraid that some may be deliberately excluded? We do not know. But at least we can see the great importance Paul gave to even the least of the brethren.

5²⁸. Paul's final prayer is that the gracious presence of the Lord Jesus Christ may be with them.

SECOND EPISTLE TO THE
THESSALONIANS

Introduction

THE second epistle stands alongside the first, with similarities and differences which present a perplexing problem. The writers are the same, and both epistles are written to '*the church of the Thessalonians*'. The same problems are mentioned or discussed—e.g. persecution, the 'Second Coming', the need for faithful work. The similarity extends to structure and language —compare, for example, the '*Finally then, brethren*' of 1 Thess 4^1 with the '*finally, brethren*' of 3^1. Yet Paul says nothing to help us understand why there are two letters. (Such a word as 'Thank you for your reply to my first letter. Here are my further comments', would have been very helpful!) But as well as the similarities there are differences. The thanks in 1$^{3-4}$ seem to be 'colder' than the thanks of 1 Thess 1$^{2, 9}$. Some have doubted whether the Jewish language and imagery of the first and second chapters of the second epistle would have been understood by the Gentiles presupposed by 1 Thess 1^9. But the chief difference is thought to be in the treatment of the 'Second Coming'. In the first epistle it is as sudden and un-advertised as a thief in the night; in the second it is to come after certain recognizable events such as the 'falling away' and the revelation of the 'man of sin'.

Some have denied that Paul wrote the second letter, chiefly because of the difficulty of fitting 2$^{1-12}$ into his theology. But in fact the combination of the suddenness of the last things with preliminary signs of their coming is a paradox frequently found in NT eschatology (e.g. in Mk 13). A 'forgery' in Paul's life-time is surely most unlikely. And if anyone had desired to write a letter and pretend it was Paul's, he would have con-centrated wholly on similarities and avoided puzzling differ-ences!

Other suggestions have been made—e.g. that *1 Thessalonians* was written for the Gentiles in the Thessalonian church and

2 Thessalonians for the Jews. (But would Paul have countenanced apartheid?!) Or that *2 Thessalonians* was written by Timothy or Silas, with Paul adding his signature. (This does not sound like Paul.) Or that *2 Thessalonians*, with its more sonorous and liturgical language, was written to be read in the meeting of the congregation for worship. On the whole the differences, though real, are not serious enough to demand a different author or a different aim.

Some have tried to date *2 Thessalonians* before *1 Thessalonians*, suggesting that it may have been written from Athens (as there is no time for a letter from Corinth before *1 Thessalonians* —see 1 Thess 3⁶). But a careful examination of the letters seems to show that the situation to which the second letter is written is later than that in the first. In particular, the problem of 'loafing', mentioned almost casually in 1 Thess 4¹¹⁻¹², has reached serious proportions in 3⁶⁻¹⁴.

So on the whole it is best to think of Paul writing the second letter not long after the first. But in the meantime he has received news—of a false idea that '*the day of the Lord is now present*' (see Comment on 2²); of an increase in 'absenteeism'; of a continuation of persecution; and also, probably, that the Thessalonians were modestly disclaiming the praise given them in the first letter. With these presuppositions the letter is reasonably intelligible!

Commentary

1^{1-2}: Greeting

THE greeting is the same as that of the first epistle, except for two small points. God the Father, the Father of our Lord Jesus Christ, is *our* Father. Grace and peace come *'from God the Father and the Lord Jesus Christ'*. So the stage is unobtrusively set for the consolation which is a marked feature of this letter. As God is our Father, He will assuredly give us His grace and peace.

1^{3-12}: Consolation for the Persecuted

We proceed on the assumption that Paul wrote this second letter soon after the first, and that in the interval he had received news, either by letter of word or mouth, of the Thessalonian church, including their reaction to his first letter. This paragraph presupposes (*i*) a humble disclaimer ('we are not worthy') of the praise in 1 Thess 1, and (*ii*) a continuation of the persecution, with consequent need for further consolation.

Summary: *Let the thought of God's coming judgement be comfort to you—and challenge.*

1^{3-4}. Paul begins again with thanksgiving. Some have seen in this thanksgiving a significant change of tone when compared with the thanksgiving of the first letter. There Paul said, 'We give thanks' (1 Thess 1^2); here he says, *'We are bound to give thanks'* (1^3). There he said, 'we need not to speak anything. For they themselves report concerning us' (1 Thess 1^{8-9}); here he says, *'we ourselves glory in you'* (1^4). The tone, it is thought, is colder, more reluctant. But this is a mistaken idea. To say, 'I am bound to do something; it is my duty' does not necessarily mean (as Indian ways of speaking, for example, abundantly show) that there is any reluctance in doing it. Time has passed since the first flush of enthusiasm of 1 Thess 1, and the event (whatever it was) which underlay 1 Thess 1^{8-9} (see comment). Paul is answering the Thessalonian disclaimer 'we are not worthy'. 'No', he says, 'it *is* meet'; 'we *are* bound'

(1³). Even now, at this interval after the first arrival of Timothy with the 'good news', we apostles often find ourselves speaking of the 'triumphs of His grace' among you! This thanksgiving does in fact contain very high praise indeed. In 1 Thess 3¹⁰, Paul had spoken of his earnest, continuous prayer to 'see your face' and 'perfect that which is lacking in your faith'. Here he gives thanks that, although his visit had not been possible, '*your faith groweth exceedingly*' (1³). In 1 Thess 3¹² he had prayed 'the Lord make you to increase and abound in love one toward another, and toward all men'. Now his prayer has been answered!—'*the love of each one of you all toward one another aboundeth*' (1³). But when Paul speaks in the churches about the Thessalonians he especially mentions their patience and faith in persecution and afflictions (which, as he hears, they still endure)—faith undefeated by persecution, and patience which triumphs over affliction.

1⁵. Paul now proceeds to consolation, in a verse which reminds us of Mt 5¹⁰, 'How blest are those who have suffered persecution for the coming of right; the kingdom of Heaven is theirs' (*NEB*). The persecutions and afflictions of the Thessalonian believers are endured 'for the kingdom'. They are God's hard way of bringing them to the kingdom. The situation is, in fact, '*a manifest token of the righteous judgement of God*'. It is not clear how these words are to be interpreted. Are the persecutions themselves the 'manifest token'—of the fulfilment of God's decree that 'through many tribulations we must enter into the kingdom of God' (Acts 14²²)? It is more likely that the token is the faith and patience of the believers in the midst of the persecution. This is a human impossibility—and therefore a sign that God is in the situation, that He has not forgotten and will not forsake His children.

1⁶⁻⁷ᵃ. The God who is now in the midst of the fire of persecution with His children is the just and righteous Judge who must one day reveal His righteousness in a complete reversal of the present situation: for those who afflict, affliction; for those who are afflicted, rest. '*With us*', Paul adds, reminding the brethren of the solidarity of God's people in suffering and in consolation.

1⁷ᵇ⁻⁸ᵃ. Again the Coming is described, now in its aspect of Judgement. The Lord Jesus will be *revealed* from heaven. His session at God's right hand is real, though hidden. At God's time He will be revealed in power and glory—with the twelve legions of angels He rejected at the time of His humiliation (Mt 26[53]); *'in flaming fire'*—in 1 Cor 3[13] the fire of judgement, here the glory of the Judge.

1[8b]. This whole section is full of OT language—see Isa 66[15–16]; Jer 10[25]. The Lord Jesus will administer God's justice (*NEB*) *'to them that know not God'* (the culpable ignorance of Rom 1[18–25]) and *'to them that obey not the gospel'* (who do not welcome the good news with obedient faith). Paul may intend Gentiles by *'them that know not God'*, and Jews by *'them that obey not the gospel'*. But we must not draw distinctions too fine. What is to be judged is that culpable ignorance of God, revealed in the rejection of the gospel—wherever it is found.

1[9]. The fate of the rejected is *'eternal destruction'*. Paul speaks not so much of the loss of existence, an idea which seems never to have occurred to the Hebrews, as of the irrevocable loss of all that makes life to be truly life—the presence, glory and power of the Lord.

1[10]. But Paul is not giving the sort of consolation which gloats over the fate of the persecutors. He turns rapidly to the glories of grace. All this will happen *'in that day'*—the day of God's choice, when the Lord shall come *'to be glorified in his saints'* and *'. . . marvelled at in all them that believed'*. Does *'in'* here mean simply 'in the midst of'? Or is there not the wonderful idea that He will be glorified in His saints because His glory has been communicated to them and is seen in them?—that He will be marvelled at because of what His grace has done in the believers?

> *Changed from glory into glory,*
> *   Till in heaven we take our place.* (*MHB* 431)

'because our testimony unto you was believed' is an awkward, but very consoling, addition. In the words *'in all them that believed'* there was implicit the thought 'among whom you Thessalonians will have a place'. Paul now makes the thought explicit—you *will* be there, for you believed.

1[11–12]. And now follows one of the wonderful prayers in which these epistles abound. In giving consolation to the persecuted, Paul must needs be honest. Necessary as suffering may be for salvation, it is not an automatic lift into the kingdom. Persecution *may* produce impatience and despair. There is need for prayer. So he prays,

(*a*) '*that our God may count you worthy of your calling*'. That calling is 'into his own kingdom and glory' (1 Thess 2^{12}). It is not a call given once for all. God is 'he that *calleth*' (1 Thess 5^{24}). The call is constant, because constantly renewed. And God is constantly at work, not only in His call, but in our response. The word translated 'count worthy' can also mean 'make worthy', as *RSV* translates, and neither meaning should be excluded. It is God's way in His grace to 'count us worthy' and then to make us to be in fact what we have by grace been counted to be.

(*b*) '*and fulfil every desire of goodness . . . with power*'. 'Desires for goodness' and 'works of faith' are often ineffectual because 'the flesh is weak'. Paul prays that God's power may bring the weak desires to effective action.

(*c*) '*that the name of our Lord Jesus may be glorified in you . . .*' Where there is hearty acceptance of God's call and full reliance on God's power, the Lord's name (i.e. the Lord's person) is glorified, as God's name was glorified in Jesus (Jn 12^{28}: see *OEE* 137); and already His glory begins to be communicated (2 Cor 3^{18}). And all this takes place, not by human striving but by grace.

For further comment on this prayer, see *Note* 19.

Note 13: Judgement

This passage sets forth God's '*righteous judgement*' (*v.* 5); and this is what we must preach. The stress here is mainly on the future aspect of God's judgement, an important part of the biblical message, but by no means the whole. There are other aspects of judgement in the passage and these also must be brought out. We need, as a basis, a brief sketch of the whole biblical concept.

'Shall not the Judge of all the earth do right?' says Abraham, unforgettably, in his prayer for Sodom. 'Far be it from Thee . . . to slay the righteous with the wicked' (Gen 18^{25}). This is a good vantage-point for a brief glance at the OT paradox of judgement. God is Judge because He is King, for judging is a function of kingly rule. But this King had bound Himself to His chosen people by a Covenant, and there is a sense in which God's righteous judgement is simply His fidelity to His Covenant-promise to be the God of His people. This means giving victory to His people over their enemies; ensuring fair treatment for the fatherless and widow among His people (Deut 10^{18}); or saving the whole people from oppression and exile (Isa 46^{13}, 51^5). This saving judgement which they experienced in history pointed forward to a Last Judgement, a 'Day of the Lord', in which God would finally and decisively vindicate His people and abolish their enemies.

But over against this OT idea there is another. God's sovereignty is not restricted to Israel, it is universal; God is not only the Merciful who hastens to save His people, but the Holy who must punish sin wherever it is found; even among His own people. And no man, even among God's people, *deserves* the Judge's favourable verdict. 'Justice is far from us' (Isa 59^9, *RSV*) because 'your iniquities have separated between you and your God' (Isa 59^2). So the prophets proclaim that the day of the Lord will be 'darkness, and not light' (Amos 5^{18}), a day not of redemption for Israel, but of destruction (Isa 5$^{1-7}$; cf. Isa 1$^{24-31}$, Mic 1$^{2-5}$).

The OT has no solution to this problem of the clash between God's holiness and His love. It simply points forward—through Jeremiah, for instance, and his new covenant; through the book of Job, where Job in his self-conscious righteousness has to meet the mysterious God in a personal encounter and learn to 'repent in dust and ashes' (Job 42^6); through Second Isaiah and the Suffering Servant. But it is this problem that Christian preaching sets out to solve. Not the academic problem of theology, but the deep problem of anxiety arising from the clash between man's need and his unworthiness—whether it be the anxiety of the Pharisee, striving to earn a redemption which must for ever elude him, or modern man who thinks he has solved the problem by repressing it and consciously thinking about it no more.

The solution is Jesus, to whom the OT pointed forward. His teaching is full of the idea of judgement, the call to repentance. It sounds forth in the Sermon on the Mount (e.g. Mt 7$^{21-7}$), the address to the disciples (Mt 10$^{28, 33}$), in parables of the Kingdom (Mt 13$^{30, 47-50}$), in parables of crisis (Mt 24 and 25), in dialogue with the crowds (Mt 11$^{20-4}$, Lk 13$^{1-5}$) or with the Pharisees (Mt 12³², 23¹³⁻³⁵). See *AMW, in loco.* All will be judged, according to the law of love. In the judgement there will be no place for human merit (Lk 17⁷⁻¹⁰); salvation will come through God's forgiveness alone. But the crucial point is not His teaching in itself. Other prophets and teachers had spoken of judgement. But Jesus is proclaimed as the One who, in answer to the question of Caiaphas 'Art thou the Christ, the Son of the Blessed?' replied 'I am' (Mk 14⁶¹, ⁶²), acknowledging Himself to be, in person, the Judge of the Last Judgement. If that is true, then history has been cut in two, the End has begun to be, *now.* So that when we see Him, with the power of the Son of Man on earth, giving God's gift of forgiveness to sinners (Mk 2⁵, Lk 7⁴⁷⁻⁵⁰) we see something of ultimate significance. This gift of forgiveness, which brought salvation to those who received it (Lk 7⁵⁰, 19⁹), provoked those who rejected His claims to make that charge of blasphemy (Mk 2⁷) which led straight to the Cross. See *CLM, in loco.*

The rest of NT teaching is the making explicit of what is contained here. Christian preaching of judgement looks back to the Cross, looks forward to the End, and directs the inter-section of beams of light from these two events upon the present. The Cross is an essential element in judgement. At the time when Jesus dedicated Himself to death and received the Father's glorifying (Jn 12²⁷⁻³²), He said, '*Now* is the judgement of this world' (Jn 12³¹; *OEE* 137). The Cross is the answer to the clash between God's holiness and His love, for it is at one and the same time both ultimate judgement *on* sin and ultimate salvation *from* sin.

The Cross, as the decisive event inagurating the time of God's judgement, and so of His victory over evil, points forward directly to the Last Judgement when His purpose will be complete.

But the preaching of judgement is not only telling an old story, or speculating about the future. It is, above all, challenge and appeal *now*—and that in three ways.

(*a*) The events of the End are brought unambiguously into the present by both John and Paul. The light has come. Men pass judgement, final judgement, upon themselves by their attitude to the Light here and now (Jn 3¹⁸⁻²¹; *OEE* 35) and the evil consequences of men's refusal to accept the Light are seen to be, here and now, God's wrath, His righteous opposition to evil (Rom 1¹⁸⁻³²; *VT* 24 f).

(*b*) In the midst of life here and now, Christian preaching offers freely and unconditionally God's forgiveness, made actual when this free, unmerited giving, which is the grace of God, is met by that utterly humble act of receiving which is faith in Christ crucified. So the sinner is justified or acquitted by the Judge, here and now, and received into fellowship with Himself.

(*c*) God's forgiveness admits a believer into a new life. But the new life in Christ is not a life entirely without judgement. Paul says paradoxically that, although justification is by faith, judgement is by works (Rom 2^{1-11}, 2 Cor 5^{10}). He means that the new life, although a life of freedom, is a life of freedom to *serve*, to *work*, to *obey*. Faith, if it is living faith, works 'through love' (Gal 5^6). If there is no evidence in the believer of what Paul, in 1 Thess 1^3, calls the 'work of faith', then that man's faith is vain. So the Christian preaching of judgement must always end in the present. We are given various pictures of the Last Judgement (e.g. Mt 25^{14-30}, 25^{31-46}, 7^{22-3}; see *AMW*). All are a challenge to live *now* a life of stewardship of the talents the Master has given; a life of love which shall be the unconscious overflow of the heart of one who is 'known by Him'. We must all appear before the judgement seat of Christ. In Christ, and by the power of the Spirit, 'we may have boldness in the day of judgement' (1 Jn 4^{17}; see *GPL* 108).

Preaching from this passage **(1^{3-10})** will stress all these elements—the gospel of our Lord Jesus, by which the believer comes to the knowledge of God and to obedience to Him (*v.* 8); the certainty of His final victory and the ultimate cleansing of the universe from sin; and the challenge now to endure affliction in His power (*v.* 4) and to allow Him to fulfil every desire and goodness and every work of faith to His glory (*vv.* 1, 12).

2^{1-17}: Wait Calmly!

(a) 2^{1-12}: *The End is not yet*

Summary: *The belief that the Day of the Lord is now present (however it arose) is false. You have not yet reached the End. You still have much to do and to suffer.*

We now come to a passage of notorious obscurity. But for Paul and the Thessalonians it was a passage of great importance, probably the main reason for the writing of this second letter. Paul had heard (exactly how and in what form we do not know) that some in Thessalonica were saying—and on his authority (in spite of what he had said in his first letter!)— 'the Day of the Lord is already here' (2², *NEB*). This was not unnaturally leading to alarm and confusion, and no doubt to the increase of 'loafing' (chapter 3). In this situation Paul gives yet another description of the Coming.

2¹. The subject is again the Coming and '*our gathering together unto him*'. This 'gathering of the elect' was a traditional concomitant of the Coming (Mk 13²⁷, 1 Thess 4¹⁷). The same word is used in Heb 10²⁵ of the weekly gathering of Christians for worship—perhaps regarded as a sign and foretaste of the ultimate gathering.

2². An obscure verse. It is reasonably clear that some at Thessalonica were saying, '*the day of the Lord is now present*'. It is not easy to see exactly what they meant by this. On 'that Day', as Paul describes it, there will be no room for disagreement as to whether it is present or not! Presumably they regarded 'the day of the Lord' as a series of related historical events, and declared that that series had now begun, so that their fulfilment would inevitably come in a brief and measurable time. It is clear that this statement had suddenly '*shaken*' and '*troubled*' the community. The real obscurity of the verse lies in the words '*either by spirit, or by word, or by epistle as from us*'. '*as from us*' must mean that the statement about the Day of the Lord was being made on Paul's authority. Is '*as from us*' to be taken with 'spirit', 'word' and '*epistle*'? If so, it will mean that something like this was said. 'Paul has said in an ecstatic utterance, in a sermon, in a letter, that the Day of the Lord is present.' It is perhaps better to take '*as from us*' only with the '*epistle*' and to think that the '*spirit*' and '*word*' happened in Thessalonica. After all, Paul has said (1 Thess 5¹⁹⁻²⁰), 'Quench not the Spirit; Despise not prophesyings'! Perhaps on hearing this the Thessalonian ecstatics and prophets 'let themselves go' in '*spirit*' and '*word*', and spoke also of a letter 'as from Paul'. This also is difficult to understand. It must mean a letter said to be from Paul which was not in fact from him. It cannot therefore refer to the First Epistle. Perhaps there was some rumour about a letter of Paul's. Perhaps, as some suggest, Paul himself did not fully know what

had happened. But no doubt we should bring 3¹⁷ into connection with this situation. Whatever had happened, Paul felt
that he must in future make sure that everyone knew which
letters were really his!

2³. Paul entirely repudiates any connection with such a statement '*in any wise*'—whether through spirit, word, letter or any
other way; to believe such a statement is to be *beguiled*. The
Day of the Lord cannot yet be present, for it must be preceded
by certain events which have not yet happened. These are

(*i*) '*the falling away*' ('rebellion' (*RSV*); 'the final rebellion
against God' (*NEB*)). The Greek word means political rebellion, but here 'rebellion against God'. The idea goes back to the
situation of the book of Daniel—the persecution under
Antiochus Epiphanes, when many Jews 'fell away'. It was
believed that this falling away would be repeated in an extreme
form in the terrible time of suffering before the End (see Mt
24¹⁰⁻¹², Rev 16⁹, ²¹). But Paul, with the Thessalonian situation
in mind, makes it very clear (see comment on *vv.* 9–12) that he
thinks of this '*falling away*' not as a falling away of believers
from the faith, but as a final rebellion of unbelief.

(*ii*) the 'revelation' of an individual described as '*the man of
sin*' (in some MSS. 'the man of lawlessness'—but 'sin is lawlessness', 1 Jn 3⁴; see *GPL* 35–6)—or 'the son of perdition'.
This means an individual whose whole nature is sin or revolt
against God, whose *fate* is perdition. He is '*revealed*', which
means that there is a supernatural agency at work in his
coming (that of Satan, *v.* 9). But we must not press the word
to mean that Paul thought of the '*man of sin*' as already
existent, awaiting the time of his revelation, as he thought of
Christ.

2⁴. The man of sin is the embodiment of human pride. He
sets himself against '*all that is called God*', i.e. against the true
God and all 'so-called gods', all objects of worship; usurping
the place of God and demanding that all worship be given to
him. There is no need to locate the '*temple*', either in Jerusalem
or in heaven. The 'man of sin' tries to take the place of God.

2⁵. With a touch of impatience Paul reminds them of his
former teaching which they have so swiftly forgotten.

2⁶⁻⁷. Now follows a very mysterious passage. The revelation of the man of sin has its '*own season*'—its own place in God's time (see comment on 1 Thess 5¹). Until God's time for his revelation comes, he is under restraint, and the Thessalonians are said to know the nature of the restraint. In *v.* 6 it is in the neuter, '*that which restraineth*'. In *v.* 7 it is in the masculine, '*one that restraineth*'. In spite of the restraint on the revelation of the man of sin, '*the mystery of lawlessness doth already work*' ('the secret power of wickedness is at work', *NEB*). This state of affairs is to last till the restraint 'is out of the way' (*RSV*).

Interpretations of the 'restraint' have ranged from the devil to the Holy Spirit. Only three need to be taken seriously. The first is based on Rom 13, and interprets the restraint as the power of the Roman Empire, or of ordained government in general. In this case '*that which restraineth*' is the State, and '*one that restraineth*', the Emperor. Paul thought highly of the State as 'ordained of God' (Rom 13¹) and might well have thought of it as God's bulwark against the inrush of the great rebellion. The second interpretation is based on Rev 20¹⁻³. In this passage, after the episode of the White Horseman, inaugurating God's final victory (Rev 19¹¹⁻¹⁶), and the destruction of the first two members of *Revelation's* 'Satanic trinity'— the beast and the false prophet (Rev 19¹⁷⁻²¹), there comes one of the Seer's characteristic 'interludes'. An angel comes from heaven with a key and a chain, with which he chains up Satan for the thousand years of the millennium. Some such mythological ideas may underlie this passage, though this explanation has no ready clue to the alternation of neuter and masculine as applied to the Restraint. The third interpretation is based on Mk 13¹⁰, where the preaching of the gospel to all nations is given a 'season' in the eschatological time-table. According to this interpretation, the 'restraining power' is the gospel, and the restrainer Paul himself! But Paul never gives any hint that he really regarded his own death as something possessing the importance he attaches to the removal of the '*one that restraineth*'. On the whole it is best to confess with Augustine that we do not know what Paul means!

2⁸. Once the Restraint has been removed, in God's good time, then the lawless one will be revealed. But Paul does not keep his readers in suspense. All will be well! In spite of all the powers of the Man of Sin, he will be slain by the Lord Jesus at His coming—by '*the breath of his mouth*' (cf. Isa 11⁴), annihilated '*by the manifestation of his coming*'. Two words are used here, both of which are used of the Coming—'appearance' and 'presence'. It seems best not to translate, with *NEB*, the 'radiance of his coming', but to think of them as synonyms. Paul's idea is that, in spite of all the powers and signs and wonders of the Man of Sin, Christ's mere presence is enough to make an end of him.

2⁹⁻¹⁰. We now return to the brief inglorious career of the Man of Sin from his revelation to Christ's appearing. He appears to be an evil parody of the Messiah. As Christ was sent by God, so is the Man of Sin sent by Satan. As Christ did mighty works as signs of the kingdom, so the Man of Sin has power to perform signs and wonders—but lying, sinful wonders. But only those are deceived by them who are already '*perishing*', on the road to destruction. And they came to be on the road to destruction because of their own choice— they '*received not the love of the truth*' which would have put them on the other road, the road to salvation. God does not put anyone on the road to destruction. He is at work in the world with His weapons of love and truth, trying to lead men to salvation.

2¹¹. But it is His own righteous decree that where the truth is deliberately rejected, the consequence shall be error and the believing of truth's opposite—the Lie, the proclamation of Satan.

2¹². The choice is before us—love of the truth and salvation, or love of sin and judgement.

Note 14: Antichrist

The Cross, as we have seen, was the *decisive* defeat of evil, but not the *final* victory of Love. The New Age was inaugurated with the Resurrection; but the old age did not then pass away. The Church lives and works in the time when the 'ends of the ages are come' (1 Cor 10¹¹), i.e. when the two ages overlap. 'Let both grow together until the harvest', said Jesus in His parable (Mt 13³⁰). The picture is of a future containing both developing good and developing evil, in tension till the End. In its thought about the coming crisis, the Early Church took over from Jewish apocalyptic the idea of 'the darkest hour before the dawn', the terrible birth-pangs preceding the wonderful birth, the last mighty effort of the devil against God, of Antichrist against the Messiah.

This passage should be compared with other 'Antichrist' passages in the NT. In Rev 13$^{1-10}$ the Roman Empire, accompanied by the priests of the Caesar cult (Rev 13$^{11-18}$) fills the role of Antichrist. In Mk 13^{14} we have a figure similar to the man of sin sitting in the temple of God—'the abomination of desolation standing where he ought not'. In 1 Jn 2^{18} the Antichrist expectation is fulfilled by 'many antichrists'—false teachers arising from the midst of the Church (see *GPL* 67 f). The description of Judas in Jn 17^{12} as 'the son of perdition' (cf. 2^3) may mean that the author saw in him the embodiment of the power of Antichrist.

What, if anything, has this to say to us today? We hardly need the figure of Antichrist to remind us that the Bible does not teach the idea of inevitable progress. But, if we cannot believe that we are getting better and better, must we believe that history is destined to get worse and worse? As we consider the movement of history we can find plenty of grounds for pessimism. Man's mastery of natural forces shoots ever further ahead of his ability to use them. His pursuit of 'peace' leads by a process from which he seems unable to escape to ever bigger stockpiles of ever more destructive weapons. His pursuit of 'freedom' is combined with increasingly effective methods of dominating and enslaving men's minds.

But we must not let the spirit of Antichrist deceive us into the idea of 'inevitable regress'. If optimism is excluded, so is pessimism. The tares are growing, but so is the wheat. The mystery of lawlessness is already at work. But so also is the Holy Spirit. As time goes on the choice before man becomes more and more clear, more and more terrible. But this passage is not a history lecture, but a stirring call to action. The Thessalonians were heaving a sigh of relief—'The day of the Lord is here. Now we can relax!' But Paul says, 'Not so! Christian, seek not yet repose! Up and put on your armour. You are to fight the mystery of lawlessness and the ever-present possibility of Antichrist.'

Antichrist is that embodiment of evil which God tells us to fight against *now*. He has been variously interpreted—as a Pope at the time of the Reformation, for example, or Hitler! These represented real dangers which the Church needed to

fight, each in his time. And so the passage challenges the
Church today—to read the signs of the times and to work, live
and pray in an urgent effort to spread 'the love of the truth'
(2^{10}). But let us not only seek for Antichrist 'outside'. Let us
not forget the antichrists who came from inside the Church
itself. The Church itself, the new life of faith, is by no means
exempt from the corruption of the demonic. Judas was 'the
son of perdition'. Jesus said to Peter, 'Get thee behind me,
Satan!' Lord, is it I?

(b) 2^{13-17}: *The Sure Hope of the Christian*
Summary: *Be comforted and stand fast. You are in His hands.*

In 1^{3-12} Paul had spoken to 'believers persecuted', setting
before them the coming great Transformation which would
cast persecutors into outer darkness and reveal persecuted
believers wonderfully glorified by grace. He prayed that this
might be true for the believers in Thessalonica. In 2^{1-12} he
faced believers all too quickly shaken and troubled by a false
report, and felt bound to remind them that things would get a
great deal worse before they got better! He knew that there
would be some, perhaps not only the faint-hearted, who at this
point would wonder whether their faith would survive through
the mystery of lawlessness and the revelation of the Man of Sin
to the glories to follow. So Paul, with understanding and love,
returns to consolation in a section which has been called 'a
system of theology in miniature'. But it is very practical
theology!

2^{13}. Here is one of the great 'buts' of grace! Terrible realities
have been disclosed—'eternal destruction from the face of the
Lord' (1^9); the 'working of error' (2^{11}) and believing of a lie,
with appropriate judgement to follow. *But*—for you we are
bound to give thanks. For whom? '. . . *brethren beloved of the
Lord*'—whom God the Father, through His love revealed in
the love of Jesus, has brought into the family of His adopted
sons, brothers to one another. And why the thanks? '*for that
God chose you from the beginning unto salvation*'. When tempted
to wonder, 'Will my faith stand?' the Christian must take refuge
in the truth that his faith is not something which rests on the
power of his human resolutions, but is part of God's eternal
plan. In His eternal counsels God chose you for salvation (and

as destruction has been defined as the eternal loss of 'the face of the Lord and the glory of His might' **(1⁹)**, salvation can be understood as the eternal sharing in these things). In some manuscripts (see *RV* margin) there is a variant reading for the word translated *'from the beginning'—aparchen* instead of *aparches*. This would mean 'chose you as firstfruits'. If this reading were accepted it would give expression to the other side of God's choice—choice not for privilege but responsibility (for 'first-fruits' are not in and for themselves, but point to the rest of the harvest). But it is reasonable that in this kind of consolation context Paul should concentrate mainly on the privilege of the choice. Yet the responsibilities are there. God chose you, not for a salvation to come automatically, without your willing or acting, but for a salvation *'in sanctification of the Spirit and belief of the truth'*. The Spirit given through Christ, and received by faith, consecrates the believer for God's service, and gives strength to translate that consecration into action. And faith is not empty emotion, but taking hold of truth, or rather trust in one who *is* Truth.

2¹⁴. So much for God's intention. In the fulness of time that intention became fact, when Paul and his companions came to Thessalonica with the good news of what God had done through Jesus Christ. In the proclamation of that gospel, God called (to privilege and responsibility) those whom He had chosen, and so set them on the road to the obtaining of the glory of the Lord in whom they had believed. *'Glory'* is the brightness of God's presence. That glory came to earth in Jesus Christ, and was revealed paradoxically and wonderfully in the Cross; see *OEE* 127. Now He is in that glory which was His before the world was. To be in Him is to share that glory, partially here, fully there.

> By faith we see the glory
>   To which Thou shalt restore us;
>   The Cross despise
>   For that high prize
>   Which Thou hast set before us. (*MHB* 411)

2¹⁵. The 'but' is followed, as usual, by a 'therefore'. All the affirmations of the preceding verses are true. What follows? ('Be not quickly shaken' but) *'stand fast'*—in persecution, false reports, and the mystery of lawlessness. And standing fast means holding '*the traditions*' preached, taught and written by Paul and his companions. There is a 'tradition of men' which must *not* be held fast (Mk 7⁸⁻⁹). But for Paul all that he had, whether preaching or teaching, was tradition—something received from the Lord (1 Cor 15³), whether directly or through His Church, and so to be faithfully passed on.

2¹⁶⁻¹⁷. Paul has set forth the gift and demand of the gospel. He proceeds to another prayer. Again, as in 1 Thess 3¹¹⁻¹³, God and Christ are addressed in their unity—separate names, but unity of action expressed by a singular verb. And here Christ is put first. God in Christ has loved us and given us the very things we need—encouragement which is not of this fleeting world but of His eternity, and hope which is 'good' (i.e. reliable), 'which putteth not to shame' (Rom 5⁵). May that God Himself apply His gifts to your situation—strengthening you in the inmost depths of your personality and giving an inner firmness revealed outwardly in actions and words which are good, like His hope.

> *O that every work and word*
> *Might proclaim how good Thou art,*
> *Holiness unto the Lord*
> *Still be written on our heart!* (*MHB* 566)

N.B. For more about this prayer, see *Note* 19.

Note 15: Election

'God chose you' (2¹³). Must we not proclaim this fact? The high mysteries of election are not the first lessons in the Christian life; they come later. When Jesus said, 'Come, follow me', He brought a man into a place of vital decision. Everything depended on whether he 'left the nets and followed' (Mk 1¹⁸) or 'went away sorrowful' (Mk 10²²). It was only later, in the shadow of the Cross, that those who had chosen Him learnt more about the real meaning of their choice—'Ye did not choose me, but I chose you' (Jn 15¹⁶). Understanding of election (to quote Thielicke) 'appears in that moment when I have struggled with the devil and my own flesh, when I have passed through the mortal conflict, engaged to the quick in the battle of God and Satan for my soul, and suddenly find myself on the side of the victorious Christ, without really knowing, and certainly not being able to explain, how I got there.'

What does the Bible say? Faced with a world in revolt and disunity (Gen 11⁹), God set in motion the history of salvation. He called Abraham (Gen 12¹⁻³), and in his descendants, delivered from Egypt, gathered to Himself, through covenant, a 'chosen people' (Ex 19³⁻⁸). The OT has three very important things to tell us about election.

(*i*) If you ask *why* God chose the Jews you will get no positive answer. *Not* because they were more numerous (Deut 7⁷); *not* for their righteousness (Deut 9⁵). The reason is hidden in the mystery of His love (Deut 10¹⁵).

(*ii*) God's choice brings not so much privileges as responsibilities. God's people are chosen for hard work; to be 'a people for others'—His 'witnesses' (Isa 43¹⁰); 'a light to lighten the Gentiles' (Isa 49⁶).

(*iii*) God's choice is not favouritism. When the chosen people said, 'Is not the Lord in the midst of us? no evil shall come upon us' (Mic 3¹¹), they were making a terrible mistake which needed again and again to be corrected by the prophets. 'You only have I known of all the families of the earth; *therefore* I will *punish* you for all your iniquities' (Amos 3², *RSV*). God's choice exposes His people to the chastening of His holy love (Deut 8⁵). The real problem of the OT is whether when the chosen people refused to do His work, God can reject them (Hos 11⁸). Out of the clash of God's faithfulness and His people's disobedience arose the idea of the 'faithful remnant'.

The NT carries on the story. Jesus is the Chosen One (Lk 9³⁵, 23³⁵). He chose twelve disciples. He Himself is the embodiment of the faithful remnant, those 'in Him' are God's chosen people, through whom He does His work in the world. As we look at the NT teaching we can say the following:

(*i*) The doctrine of election gives no ground for pride. 'God chose the weak things of the world ... and the things that are not, that he might bring to nought the things that are' (1 Cor 1²⁷⁻⁸).

(*ii*) The doctrine of election, if properly understood, does nothing to sap moral effort. As Althaus says, 'Only a faith which starts from the seriousness of responsibility and the fear of the danger of death which always hangs over us, can come to rest in the certainty of God's eternal choice.' 'He chose us ... that we should be holy' (Eph 1⁴, *RSV*); the proof that the Thessalonians are chosen is power and the Holy Ghost and much assurance (1 Thess 1⁵). *Because* the Colossians are 'chosen', they must 'put on a heart of compassion, kindness . . .' (Col 3¹²; *HKM* 50). The doctrine of election gives no false security. 'Be not highminded, but fear. For if God spared not the natural branches, neither will he spare thee' (Rom 11²⁰⁻¹).

(*iii*) The doctrine of election is communal and corporate. God chooses men out, it is true; but only to send them back into the world for service, essentially united with all others who are chosen.

The NT does *not* teach that some are chosen for damnation, even in Rom 9, the 'happy hunting-ground for Calvin's "horrible decrees" '—i.e. the idea that God, in the sovereign freedom of His election, consigns some to salvation, whatever they do wrong, and others to damnation, whatever they do right. At first sight, Rom 9¹⁴⁻²⁴ looks as if it teaches this. But chapter 9 must not be separated from chapters 10 and 11. In the whole section Paul is answering the question, 'Does the absence from the Christian Church of the Jews, God's chosen people, mean that God has broken His promise to them?' Paul gives a decisive 'No'. God is free and sovereign, so that no man, even a Jew, has any *claim* on Him (chapter 9). The Jews were in any case rejected because they *deserved* to be rejected (chapter 10). But (oh the riches of God's mercy!) this rejection is not complete and not final (chapter 11). So when Paul in Rom 9²² calls the Jews 'vessels of wrath fitted unto destruction' ('due for destruction', *NEB*; the *RSV* translation 'made for destruction' is most misleading), he does not mean that they were fitted *by God* for destruction. Their fitness for destruction is due, as he will show in chapter 10, to their own sin. But God's sovereign freedom means that He can use the opposition of the Jews, as He used the opposition of Pharaoh in the OT, for His own purposes. But these purposes, as he will show in chapter 11, are purposes of mercy, and include the Jews! All God's choices are aimed at salvation. (See *VT* 63, 73.)

On the positive side, the doctrine of election is indispensable. God calls men to tasks far beyond their power. Like the Thessalonians in this passage, they can only stand firm amidst the working of the mystery of lawlessness if they know that their Christian 'standing' depends not on their weak choices, but on God's strong choice and appointment.

So let us proclaim the mystery of election to the people God has chosen in this atomic age. God has chosen *you*—so be humble, be thankful, be obedient, beware, seek unity, be comforted, work hard!

> *A charge to keep I have,*
> *A God to glorify,*
> *A never-dying soul to save,*
> *And fit it for the sky:*

> *To serve the present age,*
> *My calling to fulfil:*
> *O may it all my power engage*
> *To do my Master's will! (MHB 578)*

Note 16: God the Holy Spirit; the Holy Trinity

In *Note* 1 we tried to give some help to preachers making sermons about God the Father and God the Son. Now, after the last reference in the Epistles to the Spirit, we ought to collect those references together and think about preaching on Whit Sunday; and after that take up the problem of what to say on Trinity Sunday.

A. There is not so much about the Spirit in these letters as in other letters of Paul; but what we have is both rich and suggestive. We have 'God, who giveth his Holy Spirit unto you' (1 Thess 4⁸). In 1 Thess 1⁵, ⁶ Paul describes the gospel-preaching at Thessalonica as coming 'not . . . in word only, but also in power and in the Holy Ghost, and in much assurance'; and as being received 'with joy of the Holy Ghost'. In the passage we have just studied 'God chose you from the beginning unto salvation in sanctification of the Spirit and belief of the truth'. Finally (1 Thess 5¹⁹) we have 'quench not the Spirit'. These passages suggest the following themes:

The Spirit is God; holy because He is holy. What God is, the Spirit is. Where the Spirit is, there God is at work, continuing to do what He has been doing from the beginning, and supremely in Christ—fulfilling His purposes. The amazing thing is that, though He is God and His victory is certain, yet He wills to carry it out through *us*. 'He giveth His Holy Spirit to you.' This is the kind of God He is—'ultimate demand and ultimate succour', who asks the impossible of us, and at the same time gives that power which can 'laugh at impossibilities and cry it shall be done' (*MHB* 561, *v.* 5).

This is the point also of 'joy of the Holy Ghost' and 'sanctification of the Spirit'. 'Joy in affliction' (1 Thess 1⁶) is a human impossibility. So is sanctification. We cannot dedicate ourselves to God (although we often speak as if we can). If we are to be 'sanctified in truth', the Spirit must unite us with Christ's sanctification of Himself (Jn 17¹⁹). Only so can we really be detached from the world, separated to God—so as to be sent back into the world. Without the Spirit we can only desire goodness and work in faith **(1¹¹)**. The Spirit can turn the desire into actuality, and the work into power.

The Spirit is active in the preaching (1 Thess 1⁵). There is no preaching without *epiclesis*, i.e. without the putting of all on the altar, and without the strong and faithful prayer which brings down the Spirit, turns the word of men into the word of God, and gives the needed assurance both to speaker and hearer. Not only on Whit Sunday, but every time we preach, we need the gift of the Spirit, which He *gives*.

And yet, as a final paradox, the dynamic power of the Almighty God can be quenched (1 Thess 5¹⁹) and rejected (1 Thess 4⁸) by human unbelief and disobedience. God's power is made perfect in weakness. He never forces the last door, but leaves us free to prefer the sterility of our self-will to the fulfilment of His purposes. This is what most urgently needs prophetic reinterpretation today. What in our life, as individuals and churches, is a quenching and rejection of the Spirit?

> *And shall we then for ever live*
> *At this poor dying rate?*
> *Our love so faint, so cold to Thee,*
> *And Thine to us so great!*

> *Come, Holy Spirit, heavenly Dove,*
> *With all Thy quickening powers;*
> *Come, shed abroad the Saviour's love,*
> *And that shall kindle ours. (MHB 292)*

B. It is sometimes said that one of the reasons for observing the Christian year is that, unless we felt some sort of obligation on Trinity Sunday, we should never preach about the Trinity, so difficult is the theme! But, if we are to be biblical, we cannot escape this obligation. We have just tried to talk about the Spirit, and have been forced to speak of the Father and the

Son. God has revealed Himself in three names—Father, Son and Spirit. We have found ample evidence of this in our Epistles. And these three are One. We have pointed out the curious signs of this in 1 Thess 3^{11} and in 2^{16}, where prayer is addressed to God the Father and the Lord Jesus Christ. The names are different, but there is only one singular verb—God and Jesus, may *He* direct, may *He* comfort and stablish.

In preaching about the Trinity we stand, as often, on a razor edge. On the one hand we are tempted to try to give a theological lecture, to reduce a mystery of faith to a tidy theory. But the Bible does not set out the developed doctrine of the Trinity, but rather the facts of God's threefold self-revelation which subsequently led to the attempts to formulate the doctrine, now, no doubt, in need of re-interpretation. But we should, as preachers, leave the doctrine to the theologians and make known what the Bible says. On the other side of the razor edge is the New Theology which, having thrown out the Trinity with 'God out there', constructs elegant formulae to explain away the biblical facts. Here is one from John Wren-Lewis: 'The meaning is not hard to express in terms which are completely intelligible today. Love when we really know it is such that the images of Fatherhood, Sonship and Spiritual Procession can all be simultaneously applied to it: in other words, unless a relationship is a three-fold unity in which every person involved performs equally the roles of initiation, acceptance or suffering, and overflowing interpretation, that relationship is something less than a genuine experience of the creative reality of love.'

Our middle course should be an attempt to show the relevance to the Christian life of the biblical facts of God's threefold revelation of Himself. 'The Trinitarian conception' (says Dr Baillie in *God was in Christ*, 159) 'is the true basis for sound Christian living.' All the fundamental realities of Christian experience reveal, so to speak, a three-fold structure. The biblical facts throw light on these fundamental realities. They in turn further illuminate the biblical facts. We touch briefly on one or two examples.

We are members of the Church. The Church is the people of God, those whom He has called for the realization in history of His purpose. The Church is the Body of Christ, redeemed by His sacrifice, united to Him as Risen Lord. The Church is the Temple of the Spirit in which the Father continues to fulfil

His purpose and to make actual His demands by means of His gift.

We are preachers. What we speak must be the word of God. The content of our message is Christ. But our words are 'the words of men' apart from the gift of the Spirit.

Christian prayer has this same structure. We speak to the Father, in the name of Christ, and in the power (Rom 8[26-7]) of the Spirit.

And the Three are One. Each of the three elements is necessary, none may be omitted, all combine. Take Bible-reading. It will not be fruitful if any of the following is lacking: an understanding that this is the record of the self-revelation of the Father; that this is the witness to Jesus (Jn 5[29]); that it can only be understood and applied in the experience of the Spirit (1 Cor 2[12-13]). Christian fellowship is only authentic when it is understood as the meeting of the children of one Father, with Christ in the midst, and the Spirit giving unity. We misunderstand the mission of the Church unless we know *three* realities—the purpose of the Father, the Body of Christ, the power of the Spirit. Such considerations illuminate what must ever remain a joyful mystery.

> *Almighty God, to Thee*
> *Be endless honours done,*
> *The undivided Three,*
> *And the mysterious One.*
> *Where reason fails, with all her powers,*
> *There faith prevails and love adores.* (*MHB* 40)

3[1-16]: Final Exhortations

With thoughts of prayer and the faithfulness of God and of the brethren, Paul begins to bring this letter to an end.

(a) 3[1-5]: *Prayer and Further Consolation*
Summary: *Pray for me, as I pray for you.*

3[1-2]. As in 1 Thess 5[25], Paul asks for prayer, but prayer more specifically related to the situation in which he finds himself at Corinth. This is prayer as Jesus taught it—not first for his own needs, but first for God's glory. In a metaphor from the games, he asks that the gospel '*may run*'—so as to be '*glorified*' (by being accepted as the word of God—in 1 Thess 2[13]—and believed). May the success which attended the Thessalonian mission attend also the Corinthian! *Then*, if God's glory is assured, may Paul and his companions be rescued from the unreasonable and evil Corinthians who will not believe themselves, nor let anyone else believe. Jewish unbelief plays, of course, a large part in Paul's thinking. In 1 Thess 2¹⁵⁻¹⁶ it had called forth prophetic denunciation. In Rom 9–11 it will lead to theological speculation. But here Paul contents himself with the brief, sad reflection that '*all have not faith*'.

3³⁻⁴. He turns from Corinth to Thessalonica again. Has he said enough to meet that difficult situation? He cannot leave them without another affirmation of faith in God and in them. God *is* faithful. He *will* strengthen you and keep you safe *from the evil one*. (This does not mean, of course, being kept safe from *suffering*. As Mother Julian said, 'He said not that we should not be tempested nor travailed nor afflicted. But He promised "Thou shalt not be overcome".') We know you *are* keeping the traditions and will continue to do so—and this is no human, wishful thinking, but part of our faith in Christ.

3⁵. And now another prayer. May God have the direction of your lives in His strong hands, and may that direction lead you to where God's love may be shed abroad in your hearts—where you may receive that victorious patience which Christ Himself inspires and achieves within you.

> *Into Thy love direct our heart,*
> *Into Thy way of perfect peace; (MHB 135)*

(See also *Note* 19.)

(b) 3⁶⁻¹⁶: *Discipline for the Loafers*
Summary: *So the problem of absenteeism is increasing! I add my precept to my example: Work! Or church discipline!*

3⁶. They are still his beloved '*brethren*'. But the situation needs an authoritative word. So Paul '*commands*', but in the name (with the authority) of the Lord. There is an 'awkward squad' in the Lord's army (see comment on 1 Thess 5¹⁴)—believers who contradict the confidence so recently expressed (*v.* 4). The faithful brethren are to '*withdraw themselves from*' ('hold

aloof from', *NEB*) all such. That means denying them the
fulness of Christian fellowship, as a means of healing discipline.

3⁷⁻¹⁰. Paul has spoken about what he preached and taught at
Thessalonica (2⁵). Now, as in 1 Thess 2¹⁻¹², he reminds them
that his instruction was not a matter of word alone. In the
matter which had now arisen, he and his companions had been
their living example. They had refused 'to accept board and
lodging from anyone without paying for it' (3⁸, *NEB*), choosing
rather a life of hard, incessant toil—although, as the Lord's
apostles, they had a perfect right to be supported by the
churches. (For more about this right, and Paul's refusal to use
it, see 1 Cor 9¹⁻¹⁸). Practice and precept had crystallized into
one devastating maxim—'the man who will not work shall not
eat' (3¹⁰, *NEB*).

3¹¹⁻¹². But now we hear that there are some who fly in the
face of all this—'idling their time away, minding everybody's
business but their own' (3¹¹, *NEB*). Paul gives them one last
chance, in which severity and love are mingled—both in the
name of Christ. They must forthwith return to a life of quiet
work and self-support.

3¹³. Now he turns to the leaders and all other members of the
congregation, and appeals to them not to be '*weary in well-
doing*'—i.e. not to follow the bad example of the loafers, or to
give them up altogether and stop doing what is for their good.

3¹⁴ᵃ. It is to be hoped that this will be enough. But if anyone
positively disobeys he is to be 'noted' ('mark him well', *NEB*).
This is a vague word, and it is not clear whether it refers to
individual or church action. The culprit is to know that his
action is disapproved, and in addition he is to be 'sent to
Coventry'—to be denied Christian fellowship.

3¹⁴ᵇ⁻¹⁵. But the treatment is remedial, a part of brotherly love.
The culprit must never be allowed to feel that he has become
an enemy. It is stern and faithful love which will make him
ashamed—and bring him back.

3¹⁶. Another final prayer closes the section relevantly. In
1 Thess 5²³ the prayer had been to the God of peace. Here it is
to the Lord who is equally the Giver of peace (1²). May He

give you this, His greatest gift, at all times (e.g. in persecution and in difficult discipline situations) and in all ways (in confident communion with Himself, peaceful relations with others, and peace of mind with which to work quietly for one another and for Him). All this will happen if '*The Lord be with you*'.

(For more about this prayer, see *Note* 19.)

3^{17-18}: Conclusion

3^{17}. Paul now takes up the pen into his own hand. He has decided, in view of the situation in 2^2 (see comment), that he will thus authenticate every letter he sends, to avoid all possibility of error.

3^{18}. His last word of farewell is the same as 1 Thess 5^{28}, except for the significant '*all*'. With all of you—persecuted, shaken, disorderly, faint-hearted, weak—whoever you may be—His grace be with you.

Note 17: Work

Here are two converging lines of thought for our preaching. One starts from John 5^{17}—'My Father worketh even until now, and I work' (see *OEE* 55). God *works*. His creating is *work*. And His rest from creation (Gen 2^3) is not to be thought of as cessation from activity. He continually preserves, judges and gives life to His creation. God's work is seen in the history of His people (e.g. Deut 11^7, Josh 24^{31}, Ps 77^{12}, Isa 5^{12}); but especially in Christ. To Him is entrusted God's work (Jn 4^{34}, 17^4) to which His 'works' bear witness (Jn $5^{20,\ 36}$, etc.)—His work of redeeming the world, completed on the Cross (Jn 19^{30}) But although, in one sense, the work of God can be done by Christ alone, in another, men may take part in it—become God's fellow workers (1 Thess 3^2—see comment; 1 Cor 3^9). This can be done through *faith*. To the question, 'What must we do that we may work the works of God?' the answer is, 'This is the work of God, that ye believe on him whom he hath sent' (Jn 6^{28-9}). By faith in Christ believers take part in 'the work of God' (Rom 14^{20}), i.e. the upbuilding of His Church for mission. The Corinthian Church is Paul's 'work in the Lord' (1 Cor 9^1). Not only Paul, but his fellow workers, in various ways, take part in 'the work of the Lord' (1 Cor 16^{10}, Phil 2^{30}). All believers are exhorted to 'abound in the work of the Lord' (1 Cor 15^{58}). So, in our epistles, mention is made of the 'work

of faith' and 'labour of love' of the Thessalonian believers
(1^{11}, 2^{17}, 1 Thess 1^3), and of those who have a position of
leadership (1 Thess 5^{13}).

> *Jesus, confirm my heart's desire*
>   *To work, and speak, and think for Thee;*
> *Still let me guard the holy fire,*
>   *And still stir up Thy gift in me.*
>
> *Ready for all Thy perfect will,*
>   *My acts of faith and love repeat,*
> *Till death Thy endless mercies seal,*
>   *And make the sacrifice complete.* (*MHB* 386)

The other line of thought starts from Gen 2^{15}, where Adam
is put into the Garden of Eden 'to dress it and to keep it'.
Work is thus declared to be God's intention for man. But in
Gen 3^{16-19} it is further declared that his work is spoiled by his
sin. Toilsomeness and frustration have entered in. Instead of
serving God's glory, man's work is now turned towards his
own selfish interest and is robbed of the value it was intended
to have. But to those who, in faith, give up their own works
and turn to God in Christ, work is restored, so far as is possible
in this present age, to what God intended it to be. Jesus was a
carpenter (Mk 6^3), Paul a tent-maker (Acts 18^3). In these
epistles, when faced with a movement away from work, Paul
lays special stress on his own example (3^8, 1 Thess 2^9). He
himself has a right, as an apostle, to be supported by the
churches (1 Thess 2^6, cf. 1 Cor 9^{1-18}). But just as Paul had set
a good example to the Thessalonians, so the Thessalonians
should set a good example of proper independence by working
with their hands (1 Thess 4^{11}) and earning their own food
(3^{12}).

> *Thine is the loom, the forge, the mart,*
>   *The wealth of land and sea,*
> *The worlds of science and of art,*
>   *Revealed and ruled by Thee.*
>
> *Then let us prove our heavenly birth*
>   *In all we do and know,*
> *And claim the kingdom of the earth*
>   *For Thee, and not Thy foe.* (*MHB* 949)

The point is that the Bible makes no distinction between the 'Church work' of the first part and the 'work in the world' of the second part of this note. In the whole range of his life the believer is to walk in the good works which God has prepared, for which he has been created (see Eph 2^{10}). The work of the Christian, whatever it may be, is to be done 'from the heart, rendering service with a good will as to the Lord' (Eph 6^{6-7}, *RSV*), done 'to the glory of God' (1 Cor 10^{31}).

> *While in the heavenly work we join,*
> *Thy glory be our whole design,*
> *Thy glory, not our own;*
> *Still let us keep our end in view,*
> *And still the pleasing task pursue,*
> *To please our God alone.* (*MHB* 670)

Christians are to be good stewards of God's gifts of time, talents and possessions (1 Cor 4^{1-2}, Mt 25^{14-20}), and servants of their neighbours (Gal 5^{13}, 1 Pet 4^{10}). And the Paul of Thessalonians would especially wish the believer to remember that he must work in such a way that his work may stand firm in that Day when 'each man's work shall be made manifest' (1 Cor 3^{13}).

> *O that each in the day*
> *Of His coming may say:*
> *I have fought my way through,*
> *I have finished the work Thou didst give me to do.* (*MHB* 956)

Note 18: Discipline

Church discipline is not a subject often preached about, at least in Western countries. The situation is different in the 'younger churches'. When a missionary goes from the West to a country such as India he encounters, probably for the first time, a situation in which Church discipline *has* to be taken seriously. From there he probably looks back with surprise at the life of the 'gathered churches' from which he has come—churches content to let their disciplinary machinery rust, to cover up faults with decent reticence, to write 'ceased to meet' with a regret not unmixed with relief. But when, in a land like India, a believer comes by baptism from traditional social disciplines and sanctions into the Church, the Church has a

responsibility it cannot evade to replace those disciplines and
sanctions by something better. In India there is no 'decent
reticence'. Irregularities in Church life cannot be hid and must
be dealt with, if the whole work and witness of the Church is
not to be gravely compromised. And once a man becomes a
Christian, and so long as he retains the name, he is within the
Church's responsibility, even if he does 'cease to meet'. The
Church in such circumstances has to try to find a form of
discipline both true to the Bible and relevant to the contemporary situation. So sermons on 3^{14-15} are more likely to be
heard in India than in England. '. . . *note that man*' (says Paul,
addressing the whole Church body. 'Don't hide the fault in
"decent reticence" ') '. . . *have no company with him*' (take appropriate disciplinary action) '*that he may be ashamed*' (come
to repentance and return to the faith); '*yet count him not as an
enemy but admonish him as a brother*'. The essentials are here,
and are confirmed by other 'discipline' passages, such as 1 Cor
5 and Mt 18^{15-20} (*AMW* 111).

Church discipline is not an activity of 'casting down' over
against the activity of 'building up' (2 Cor 10^8, 13^{10}). It is a
part of the 'building up', just as God's wrath and judgement
are aspects of His love. So discipline must be done in humble
love and in fear and trembling (remembering Mt 7 and Gal 6^1).
Church discipline is a part of evangelism. Its aim is 'to gain
thy brother' (Mt 18^{15}), to 'save his spirit' (even that of the
incestuous man—1 Cor 5^5). Those who refuse discipline are
to be 'to thee as the Gentiles and the publican'—the objects of
especially loving care to Jesus and the early Church.

Church discipline is an activity essential to the health and
salvation of the Church itself and its members (1 Cor 5), and
it is the responsibility not only of Church leaders but of all
Christians. But how are we to interpret and exercise it in the
contemporary situation in Britain? All the emphasis today is on
the Church as 'the accepting community' (See Bishop Robinson's *The New Reformation*; 46–53). In a booklet entitled
'Anxiety—A challenge to the Church?', a psychologist writes
of the dire need for the kind of caring community in which
people can bring things out into the open and know that the
problems and revelations will be received in Christian love.
Our 'decent reticence' and 'social respectability' have brought
shallowness and unreality into our Church life. People go to
the psychiatrist instead of to the minister or the class leader. Yet

surely the Methodist church, of all churches, has the tradition
of fellowship in which this kind of healing could take place.

> *Kindly for each other care;*
> *Every member feel its share.* (*MHB* 720)

> *Together travel on*
> *And bear each other's pain;*
> . . . .
> *And join with mutual care*
> *To fight our passage through.* (*MHB* 716)

May it not be that the 'accepting community'—in which not
only theological doubts but also moral problems and sins can
be shared in an atmosphere of Christian love—is one side of
the coin, and Church discipline the other? The two belong
together. Would it not be good if the Church in the West
moved to pay new attention to both these complementary
aspects of the Christian life?

Note 19: The Six Prayers

With 3^{16} we complete our study of the six prayers of Thessalonians. We must now take another look at them, and ask
what they have to tell the preacher of today about his prayer-
life, his message and his conduct of worship. First, a brief
résumé, on the basis of the commentary—

(1) 1 Thess 3 $^{11-13}$

The prayer is kindled by abounding love. It explodes as honesty
and hope make contact, the honesty which is soberly aware of
'Satanic hindrances' (2^{18}) and the falling short of faith (3^{10});
the hope which puts no limit to what God can do. There is
mystery and depth about the prayer. Paul addresses a God
mysterious in plurality and unity (cf. 2^{16}). He is as specific in
asking (for direction of the way—3^{11}) as he will be unperturbed
if the answer is 'No' or 'Not yet'. With incredible boldness he
prays for perfection—Thessalonian hearts made firm in holiness which the Lord Jesus will pronounce faultless (*NEB*) when
He comes. But this is no pious apocalyptic fancy. What he is
praying for is abounding love *now*, within the church and for
the world.

(2) 1 Thess 5$^{23-5}$

This prayer must be seen as the climax of the second part of the letter, the means by which its teaching on purity, work, hope, watchfulness, sobriety and edification is to break forth into life. The prayer is hemmed in by thoughts of the unquenched Spirit (5^{19}), faith in God's faithfulness (5^{24}) and humility (5^{25}). Again we are taken to the heights of courageous hope. But again the hope is securely grounded in the reality of the here and now. Paul prays not for exalted states of the soul, but for perfect health of the whole personality, spirit, soul and body. And the personality, we can be sure, can only be healthy *then* if it answers the *present* call (5^{24}) of the God of peace, and fully exercises spirit, soul and body in His work of peace-making *now*.

(3) 2 Thess 1$^{11-12}$

Paul soberly faces the realities and temptations of persecution, and then sets them in the light of the blazing glories of grace. Impossible as it may seem, a day is coming when the glory of the Lord Jesus at His coming will be increased by marvel at what He has done in the Thessalonians (1^{10}). But once again the prayer brings the light of the coming glory to bear on the present. In and under the persecution is the reality of God's *call*. The Lord Jesus who is to be glorified *then* wills to be glorified *now*, as that call is answered and Thessalonian believers put themselves and their weak desires and unfulfilled works on the altar, and trust to His power to transform weakness into fulfilment.

(4) 2 Thess 2$^{16-17}$

Here again we have the same pattern. The prayer sets out from the difficult present. The mystery of lawlessness doth already work. It is necessary to stand fast and hard to do so. So we turn to what God has done and will do, His eternal comfort and good hope. But the spiritual boomerang unfailingly returns! Good hope for the future means good works and words *now*.

(5) 2 Thess 3^5

This and the last prayer hammer home with two final blows the truth that, in the words of Peter (1 Pet 3^{15}) the hope that is in us (of which the letters speak) is to have its reasons *now*.

He is living Lord. If you allow Him, He will take over the direction of your life, and steer you now into the love of God and His own patience. And this patience, to quote Barclay, is 'the spirit that can bear things not simply with resignation but with blazing hope; not the patience which grimly waits for the end, but the patience which radiantly hopes for the dawn.'

(6) 2 Thess 3[16]

The second prayer was addressed to the God of peace, who made peace through Christ. This prayer is to the Lord of peace through whom peace was made. May He give, in ways adequate to *all* your circumstances, His multifarious gift of peace. Not, of course, a gift to keep to yourself, but to give away in constant peace-making.

The Church needs preachers who will pray for those to whom they preach as Paul prayed here—with constancy, honesty, realism, relevance, humility, depth, boldness, faith, hope and love.

The message of the prayers must be proclaimed, not only in sermons, but in the whole conduct of worship. Sermons must make the ultimate demand and the ultimate offer which these prayers presuppose. But this is not enough. Our worship must reflect the whole movement of these prayers—from the temptations and sufferings of the present; to the certainties of what God has done and will do; and out again, strengthened by grace, to the difficult present. The Lord says, 'Come', and gathers His people together. Through word and sacrament He challenges, demands, feeds, gives. Then He says, 'Go, into all the world' and scatters His people into the world to show forth His power in love and obedience, in good word and work, in love, patience and peace.